How to Keep Operating in a Crisis

How to Keep Operating in a Crisis

Managing a Business in a Major Catastrophe

James Callan

GOWER

Published by
Gower Publishing Limited
Gower House
Croft Road
Aldershot
Hampshire GU11 3HR
England

Gower
131 Main Street
Burlington
Vermont 05401–5600
USA

James Callan has asserted his right under the Copyright, Designs and Patents Act 1988 to be identified as the author of this work.

British Library Cataloguing in Publication Data
Callan, James
    Business continuity planning : what to do before, during
    and after crises hit
    1. Crisis management
    I. Title
    658.4'056

ISBN 0 566 08523 2

Library of Congress Control Number: 2002101190

Typeset in 11 on 13 Plantin Light by Bournemouth Colour Press, Parkstone and printed in Great Britain by MPG Books Ltd, Bodmin.

Contents

Preface

CRISIS MANAGEMENT AND BUSINESS CONTINUITY PLANNING

Modern crisis management developed from the need to control the consequences of disaster situations in order to fulfil economic, social and political aspirations for growth and stability. Corporations, particularly those liable to public confrontation, have learned from well publicized disasters and the seemingly endless string of accidents during the last two decades that there is a need to develop a structured corporate preparedness, capable of dealing with complex disaster events. The uncertainty of secondary corporate impact, and the need for damage limitation planning to protect against loss of public image and market confidence in an increasingly litigious society, is all too frequently forgotten and has resulted in a number of large corporate failures of spectacular proportion. Many such failures can only be attributed to the inability of board level management to recognize the advantages of honest admission of liability before public scrutiny and a willingness to undertake all possible steps, irrespective of cost, to recover the situation and thereby retain corporate integrity and public confidence.

As a result of the numerous disasters during the 1980s and 1990s, governments, ecological groups and the public have hardened their attitudes towards those businesses which pay only lip service to safety, or damage the environment for extra profit or in the name of progress. It must be recognized that the management of risk, crisis and disaster can no longer be regarded as merely an 'add on' but should be integrated into a multi-discipline, crisis management culture that combines the adverse events of corporate experience into the analysis of risk.

PREPAREDNESS

Crisis preparedness is achieved by analysing threat and risk, prioritizing them, assessing their impact, and determining those corporate, technical and staff resources necessary to defuse a crisis before it reaches unmanageable criticality.

AUDIT

A 'crisis audit' will assess the level of corporate preparedness and will pinpoint areas of potential weakness. A lack of such an audit is apparent in many disasters and this can lead to trial by media which may highlight shortcomings not previously found or resolved and may suggest that financial considerations are major action inhibitors and take precedence over human life or the environment.

A review of corporate weakness, together with assistance from independent advisors and the emergency services, will help uncover areas of risk that have not previously been considered. It may seem logical to suggest that companies should study previous incidents in order to learn from them, but in fact this happens only rarely. The preparedness of organizations to deal with crises at this stage depends upon core corporate ethos, the structure and strategy of the company, and whether senior management is prepared to give full support to a crisis management team.

Despite good and effective business continuity planning, experience has shown that progressive and damaging complexities can occur in disaster situations where appropriate senior management support or involvement is missing.

PURPOSE OF THIS BOOK

This book is simply intended to be a practical 'nuts and bolts' guide to what should be included in a successful business continuity plan for an essentially office-based environment.

There is no attempt to discuss in-depth theoretical aspects of any kind, whether these be methods of risk analysis, external threat or business resilience.

ABOUT THE CD

The CD which accompanies this book has been designed to make the information contained within *How to Keep Operating in a Crisis* as useful and accessible as possible. On it you will find a range of template forms to be used when building and maintaining a business continuity plan. The pages concerned are marked ⊙ in the book. The CD also provides access to Acrobat Reader 5. In order to install the Acrobat Reader, double-click on the icon rp500enu, when prompted click on Next, and when prompted click on Next unless you wish to install to a different directory. In that case click on Browse and choose alternative location. Finally when prompted click OK. Once opened, the boxes within the forms can be filled in on screen and printed off to create a plan specific to your circumstances.

Introduction

Commercially available business continuity (BC) plans are often excessively complicated as a result of an attempt to include every aspect of business functionality in a multiplicity of disaster situations and for a wide range of business types whether commercial or industrial. In addition, emphasis may be placed on highly dramatic, but statistically infrequent events, such as terrorist attacks, without relating the benefits of mutually useful protective measures to the more mundane and frequently occurring events that are equally disruptive.

Conversely, in an attempt to rationalize this problem of complexity, some authors attempt to produce a generic text, frequently more theoretical than practical, which may give little real insight into how the 'nuts and bolts' of an effective working BC plan are assembled.

The following text details essential areas of business functionality; practical methods of incident avoidance and protection; business continuity and recovery; site recovery and salvage, together with the underlying infrastructure needed to make the plan work. It is intended as a practical package of protective measures for use across office-based business environments and has been used within financial institutions.

This book (and the BC plan) is divided into three main parts:

- **Part 1 Incident Avoidance and Mitigation**
  Those measures, whether they form constructional requirements, defensive systems, training or procedures, which are designed to either avoid a serious incident or minimize the effects of such an incident. All measures are discussed in detail in order to provide a reasoned process, enabling readers to better modify the plan for their own specific workplace environments.
- **Part 2 Business Continuity**
  The procedures and practices that will minimize the effects of a major incident on both staff and business functionality, as well as restore it in accordance with a predetermined plan and time scale. In order to facilitate use of the material there is some overlap between Parts 1 and 2.
- **Part 3 Site Recovery and Salvage**
  The protection of the damaged site. The salvage and recovery of essential materials, documentation and equipment.

To be effective, a *business continuity plan* must be a living document. Constant update and revision is an essential element and reflects the evolution of the business it is designed to protect. It is incumbent upon corporate management to instil the necessary enthusiasm and impetus if a truly effective plan is the goal. Staff must regularly review departmental requirements, make necessary changes and suggest general improvements to the BC documentation as a whole.

In order to write this BC plan, it has been necessary to assume that various items of equipment, systems, procedures or training are, or will be, in place. However, while this may not always be the case within the wide scope of business operations, there are certain protective requirements that are common to all and, if these remain incomplete, the entire protective system could fail to function.

Part 1

Incident Avoidance and Mitigation

Section 1

Overview

1.1 PLANNING

Business continuity planning is critical to corporate survival. It ensures that a business is able to continue its operations and recover its full earning ability as quickly as possible following a major disruptive incident. Planning must accommodate as many emergency situation scenarios as possible, involving as many corporate sites as may be considered necessary to maintain business functionality. It is necessary to always assume a 'worst case scenario' as this will allow at least some recovery from anything less than total destruction. This will inevitably result in some degree of overkill in a less than total destruction situation but is more cost effective and simpler to administer than a layered response.

Part 1 of this plan is concerned with what should be undertaken in order to avoid a major disruptive incident or minimize the worst effects should such an event be unavoidable.

1.2 THREATENING EVENTS

The range of events which normally threaten business functionality include:

- major fires
- electricity cuts
- gas leaks or explosions
- terrorist bomb attacks
- abrupt flooding
- transport accidents.

While there are a myriad possible incidents, they all have factors in common:

- exclusion from operational premises or facilities
- exclusion from data or records
- a reduction or cessation of productive capability
- a likely loss of staff.

1.3 EFFECTS

Any of these events can cause enormous disruption to business. Statistics have shown that without a fully operational business continuity (BC) plan, and the necessary trained staff to support it, businesses suffering major incidents are unlikely to fully recover and reach the pre-event projected level of expansion within a ten-year period. Full 'knock-on' and secondary side effects of incidents are rarely taken into consideration when overall losses are calculated, but the overall average exceeds nine times the property reinstatement value. A recent study reported that over 40 per cent of businesses with either single site premises, or those with insufficient diversification of sites, fail totally following a major incident. A further 30 per cent of the survivors also fail within the next two years.

1.4 CORPORATE BURDEN

Despite the possibility of such enormous losses it is not uncommon for the financing of contingency measures to be seen as an unnecessary corporate burden resulting in few protective measures being undertaken. Even the spread of loss by means of suitable insurance cover, such as property and capital equipment replacement or business continuity facility provision, is frequently ignored or values are under-insured to save premium costs.

1.5 RISK MANAGEMENT

The ultimate test of BC risk management skill is the ability to effectively balance risk and probability against potential financial loss and a BC budget. It is therefore an important prerequisite to identify and quantify potential risk, determine the level of preparedness and speed of recovery required, and balance this against the level of cost. No such compromise would, of course, be ethically acceptable where it impinged on the safety of staff, the public or indeed the environment.

1.6 SENIOR MANAGEMENT COMMITMENT

Senior management commitment is essential to the viability of a BC plan, and this group must provide sufficient budget to facilitate the level of BC planning, implementation and testing they have deemed necessary to support the business functionality and meet their environmental responsibilities. Staff must also be given sufficient time to establish a competent system of planning, to document implementation procedures, conduct plan testing and attend training courses. Training should involve as many departments within the business as is reasonable, in order to ensure that key functions or processes are not overlooked. However, it is realistic to acknowledge and plan for the operational cessation of some departments immediately post-disaster and for the reality that most departments will work with a reduced staff strength for varying predetermined periods. The commitment of senior management is therefore not only essential to the business recovery process but also to the support of those who do not see themselves as being an immediate part of this process. Senior management must be seen to promote BC planning at every stage and take part in essential testing when necessary. Failure to do so will inevitably produce a poor plan with lack of staff preparedness, a waste of allocated budget and severe business vulnerability.

Physical protection measures

2.1 ACCIDENTAL CAUSES OF BUSINESS INTERRUPTION

Fire is the main accidental (and deliberate) cause of business interruption in corporate premises, while, to a much lesser degree, so are power failure, flooding and gas leakage. While most are preventable by means of careful adherence to maintenance, staff training practices, incident avoidance, control practices and security, the obvious exception is the spread from neighbouring properties. Power cuts can result from generating or supply equipment failure, but are more frequently a knock-on effect of fire or flood, requiring power to be turned off, which may cause business interruption to spread over extensive areas. Businesses which are in multiple tenancy properties are potentially at much greater risk than those which are sole occupants of comparable premises. This is because they are neither in a position to control the entire environmental envelope in which they operate nor effectively isolate themselves from incidents caused by others operating within the same property.

2.2 FIRE PROTECTION

All commercial premises should be fitted with modern fire detection systems which are fully 'addressable', which means the control panel will identify exactly which device has activated and hence locate the site of any fire. Systems are normally required to activate local bells at the premises, but are usually connected to a central monitoring station so that both the fire brigade and corporate keyholders can be informed immediately when an incident occurs.

Addressable fire systems can be used to monitor other devices in addition to the more common smoke detectors, rise of temperature detectors and break-glass call points. The following are examples:

- a very sensitive vapour sampling and detection system, frequently used in ceiling and floor voids, particularly in computer departments
- a floor void sampling system which detects water

- a sprinkler system
- gaseous fire suppressant systems (as found in computer suites).

All such systems can be signalled separately from a fire system to a central monitoring station, thereby allowing the identification of a fire, flood or other problem at an early stage.

2.3 POWER FAILURE AND UNINTERRUPTED POWER SUPPLIES (UPS)

While power loss as a result of supply or transmission failure is rare in large cities, it can occur as a result of a major fire or flood which requires power termination at sub-station level while emergency services complete their operations. In smaller business areas, power failure may be more common and result from bad weather damaging power transmission equipment. There are few realistic alternative options available and while some premises have standby generators, they are rarely of sufficient capacity to carry the load of heating, lighting and air conditioning, nor of sufficient stability to be used with computer equipment unless expensive protective systems are incorporated. City requirements of safety, environmental cleanliness and noise limitation increasingly frown on the use of diesel generators running continuously or the storage of large quantities of fuel close to or within a business premises.

Standalone uninterrupted power supplies (UPSs) offers the only effective maintenance and protection of power available to the average business. Effectively, a UPS is a battery system which is connected between the existing power supply and the piece of equipment being served. The batteries are constantly charged by the supply and the item of equipment is powered via the batteries. Once the mains power supply is terminated, the equipment is supplied from the batteries, which then begin to discharge. The equipment will remain running until the batteries run out and this is dependent upon the load being taken from the batteries and their capacity. UPS systems, while available with considerable capacity, are not practical for either very high rates of discharge nor over extended periods of use. They are most effective in protecting computer systems from voltage fluctuations and allow a graceful download of data when power failure takes place.

In the event of a long-term mains power failure at any site, there would be little alternative but to abandon operations (known as exclusion) and, upon invocation, transfer operations to a business continuity emergency facility which is often known as a 'hot start site'. This should be far enough away from the affected site to be on a different power sub-station.

2.4 FLOODING

Even relatively minor levels of flooding are likely to require the termination of power and the subsequent loss of both communications and computer systems. Invocation of BC plans would need to take place and a return to the effected site would be dependent upon the ability of contracted emergency pumping and cleaning services to cope and for services to be reinstated. Extensive underfloor water-sensitive cable, can give a valuable early warning of likely flooding problems.

2.5 GAS LEAKAGE

For all practical purposes, a suspected gas leak must be considered as a 'bomb about to detonate' and staff must be evacuated with all possible speed. Individual businesses must decide how best to notify their staff that they should evacuate the premises, as the slightest spark from a personal address (PA) system, fire alarm or even telephone activation may initiate a gas explosion. It is possible to install emergency warning systems in a gas-tight form but these are uncommon outside of the chemical or petrochemical industries and other businesses would need to assess their risk potential before deciding on a suitable method of staff warning.

2.6 BOMBING – BLAST PROTECTION

Serious bomb damage, not amounting to building destruction, is likely to result from external blast. The greatest damage to staff and equipment is likely to be caused by flying glass. Very effective protection from the secondary effects of blast is obtained by the use of anti-blast film and/or blast curtains on windows, glass door panels and partitions. There should be no attempt to cut costs by the use of thin film on upper windows, as experience has shown that windows at the top of high-rise buildings can suffer as much destruction as those on lower floors in a blast situation.

2.7 PREMISES

As there is unlikely to be sufficient free space, it is probably not a realistic option for the average business to relocate staff from a damaged site into other existing operational sites, and the need for designated alternative accommodation, suitable for the purpose of business reinstatement, is therefore essential. Should further accommodation be required, standby contracts with hotels can provide adequate short-term conferencing and client meeting point facilities. Some departments will wish to make their own plans for the use of hotel facilities when dealing with clients and this may well be acceptable provided that BC administration is informed of the proposed location and details of the staff to be housed there. There are a number of concerns to be considered when using such premises for business purposes and these may include health and safety and insurance cover.

Guarding and notification of incident

3.1 NOTIFICATION OF AN INCIDENT AND ALARM ACTIVATION

During normal business hours there is rarely any difficulty with satisfactory dissemination of information whether to individual members of staff or to BC administration. However, considerable problems can arise at night, at weekends or during public holidays. If the site is staffed on a 24-hour basis by either employees or guards, there is a requirement for representatives to be made aware of the actions they should take in an emergency situation and whom they should inform. To make this possible and effective, a means of communication, such as a mobile telephone, is essential as is a regularly updated telephone call-out list, call testing and maintenance procedure.

When a site is unstaffed outside of normal working hours, there may be a need to use the facility provided by both intruder and fire alarm systems for purposes of notification. In addition to the designed activation parameters of each system, they are likely to be activated should an explosion occur. Both alarm types operate by incorporating automatic telephone systems which alert a 24-hour call centre or 'central station' belonging to the alarm company concerned. These in turn notify either the police or fire brigade, who will attend. There is the facility for call centres to be given a list of additional emergency numbers, usually called 'keyholder' lists, and this may include both a manned guarding company as first response as well as members of corporate staff. Once again there is the need to ensure that such lists are constantly updated and the call system tested regularly.

3.2 CORPORATE SITES

Each site, with its specific facilities and requirements should be documented in detail, and the following are examples:

1 There is no out-of-hours guard system at Site A. Notification of an incident would be via guards at the adjacent Site B (telephone number), or from

central station to designated keyholders following activation of the fire or intruder alarm system.

2 There is no out-of-hours guard system at Site C, nor any adjacent guarded site. Any incident can only be notified via activation of the intruder or fire alarm systems. However, the closed circuit television (CCTV) link between Sites B and C and monitored by Site B guards would indicate any damage or unusual activity. The guard would be supplied with appropriate site instructions and call-out procedures for appropriate keyholders and/or emergency services.

3 There is no out-of-hours guard system at Site D, neither are there adjacent guard sites, nor CCTV systems and the site is too remote for members of staff to attend out of normal business hours. Any incident taking place would need to activate the intruder or fire alarm system before the emergency services or first keyholder – a designated security company – could be notified to attend. All necessary sets of keys and alarm reset codes would need to be made available to the guarding company and updated when necessary.

Terrorist threats

4.1 DEVIANTS

The terrorist's bomb, the arsonist's incendiary device, the militant protester or the vandal – there is no potential shortage of these deviants operating, whether as groups or individuals, in the main cities of almost any country in the world. However, it would be realistic to say that only a minority of businesses operating in Western Europe carry a particular risk potential greater than any other when operating from well maintained business premises. Such threats that there are will either be random or the result of operating within a close proximity to businesses or environs such as embassies, which may carry a higher risk and for which special protective measures are required. It must be taken into consideration that, for those businesses with few operational sites, a greater proportion of vital resources, company records and staff are housed in each, with the resultant potential for critical business loss should a single site be destroyed.

4.2 THE THREAT POTENTIAL

Businesses that trade in arms, furs, perform animal experiments or are seen to damage the environment attract media attention, frequently court public disapproval and are the object of direct action by various active factions. Such businesses are usually well aware of their potential vulnerability to terrorist-type action. Private intelligence services will usually provide information on the current ebb and flow of threat levels and public opinion. In real terms it may be very difficult for the ordinary private business to attempt an assessment of the many active organizations or radical protest groups capable of making a threat and carrying it out. Therefore, if there is some doubt whether a particular product, service or material supplier, or indeed neighbouring company, could cause a threat situation, a detailed assessment of the business operation itself by those with a detailed knowledge of active dissident factions and both current political and economic affairs is necessary. It is probably accurate to assume that all major cities are potential targets for terrorism at some time and therefore all premises and persons working in cities are under some level of threat, whether that be as a result of business activity, geographic location or chance – as the events of 11 September 2001 have sadly shown. However, while the threat varies from time to time, it is generally still low in Western Europe and North America.

4.3 THE THREAT SOURCE

These are usually made by telephone, and on rare occasions by anonymous letter. The practice of the IRA, for example, has been to inform a newspaper, news agency or the police and give a code word to verify their identity. The threats are always routed via police and thence to the intended business premises. To date IRA call length is never more than 15 seconds, the calls so far have always been made by men and the location and time of detonation (usually 30 minutes) are always given but are often unreliable. Many groups carry out similar identification methods.

Police assess the threat and will advise, if time permits, those businesses under threat and the likely threat potential. Police have the authority to evacuate public areas, but they do not necessarily have the power to evacuate a private building unless there is a real danger to life.

Telephone calls directly from a bona fide terrorist or radical protest group to an intended victim have been rare in the past, but more recently have been used by members of animal rights groups as a method of intimidating both individuals and their families. While on the British mainland the vast majority of such calls remain hoaxes, there is no golden rule and all must initially be dealt with as if they were real threats.

4.4 DEALING WITH A THREAT

4.4.1 Direct from a terrorist to a company switchboard

The receipt of a threat message by a switchboard operator is rare, but this has become a feature of some animal rights groups. Should it occur, it is more likely to relate to an incident that is about to take place elsewhere or be a hoax. The switchboard operator MUST ensure that the correct action is taken and this consists of:

- recording the actual content of the message accurately and without delay
- passing the information to senior management (see Section 4.5 below headed 'Following receipt of a threat').

It has long been the practice to recommend that switchboard operators complete a questionnaire during a threat call. A much more realistic alternative is for switchboards to be fitted with a recording facility for selected incoming calls, but it is necessary to ensure that use of such a system does not contravene any data protection legislation. A list of questions which could be asked should the opportunity arise (see Appendices 1 and 2) should still be available, but usually such threat calls are very short (12 seconds or less) during which time the threat message is read out without any opportunity for two-way conversation.

4.4.2 From police to company switchboard

Police will try to inform all businesses, within a potential incident area, either personally, by phone or by a dedicated pager* that a bomb or other threat has

---

*The City of London Police operate an emergency pager system through which they can inform subscriber businesses of potential incidents. Where this system is in operation the switchboard and key business continuity staff should be issued with a receiving pager. A cascade list of key staff should be held by switchboard operators who can disseminate information as required.

been received, either directly or via a press agency. As, in either case, the information will have been assessed before being passed on, all such threats should be regarded as 'will happen' rather than 'may happen' and appropriate steps taken. Should such threat information be received direct from a press or similar agency the threat will be assumed as genuine and acted upon as if received from police. It should be confirmed that the press agency will inform police.

As any such warning is likely to give minimal prior notification of an incident, and even this has proved to be notoriously unreliable, information must be passed to the person deemed responsible for assessing the necessary action without delay.

4.4.3 By post

A threat received by post is uncommon, but when it does occur, it may be addressed to an individual senior member of staff. The letter, opened by a secretary or personal assistant, should be preserved *at this time* for fingerprints, handwriting and other forensic tests – not after it has been handled and examined by various staff members. The letter and envelope should be preserved in a clear plastic bag where it can be read without removal. It should be kept safely and the police should be notified immediately. The information contained within the letter should be acted upon as if it were a telephone call. For obvious reasons, a postal threat is unlikely to give a specific time of an incident, but it should still be dealt with as quickly as possible.

4.4.4 Hoax bomb threats

Hoax bomb threats are a 'legitimate' component of the terrorist arsenal and designed to cause major disruption at least cost to the terrorists themselves. There are methods of determining whether threats may or may not be hoaxes and initially this relies on the switchboard operator's ability to record the incoming threat call whether electronically or manually. However, assessment is the responsibility of the police and initially all threat calls should be actioned as real incidents.

4.5 FOLLOWING RECEIPT OF A THREAT

4.5.1 Switchboard to pass information to senior management

Upon receipt of a threat call to the switchboard, the operator should immediately inform the person responsible for the activation of emergency procedures. The chance of being able to contact an individual senior member of staff at a moment's notice must be recognized as a weakness in such a plan. A more suitable system would be the installation of an emergency conference call telephone system that would ring simultaneously in the offices and on pagers or mobile phones of all senior BC management, at all predetermined business locations. Upon any *one* person answering an emergency telephone, the operator would advise that a threat had been received and either play the recorded message or repeat that which has been written down.

The conference call line would be left open, the recipient of the call would make a 'best judgement' decision and inform the switchboard operator what action is to be taken. The message should be short and passed to all staff via an emergency public address system, which must be audible to all members of staff and the public in the premises concerned. Such a facility is considered a prerequisite to facilitate the dissemination of all emergency instructions. Once the switchboard has announced that evacuation is to take place, the public address should sound a distinct evacuation tone, which cannot be confused with the fire alarm or any other emergency notification. Once completed, the switchboard staff must evacuate the premises.

4.5.2 Inform the persons responsible for overall security

Because it is essential that there is no delay in the dissemination of information from the switchboard, it is critical that sufficient shared-number emergency telephones, mobiles or pagers will always be available and staffed. This will ensure that: (i) someone of authority and with the required knowledge is always available; and (ii) there is only ONE emergency telephone number to call.

4.5.3 Policy decision concerning evacuation

If police are convinced that there is an imminent and real threat of a bomb exploding they can insist upon immediate evacuation of premises in order to preserve life. However, they do not always invoke their power against private premises when based solely on a threat call. Hence, for those remaining within premises which subsequently come within a cordon, there is a very real danger of being trapped until the cordon is removed.

When police do not enforce evacuation, the decision is the responsibility of the company concerned. The alternatives, as discussed below, are not easy to assess and the decision rests with the senior person(s) available. This is the point at which the tape recording of the threat conversation, or the notes made by the telephone operator at the time, are so important and will invariably help senior staff produce a rapid and balanced decision based on the information available.

Specific points that may aid the decision process are as follows:

1 the likely validity of a threat call from the style of speech, intonation, stress, urgency, attitude and general approach of the caller;
2 recent history of bomb or other threats, whether they have been genuine or otherwise, both locally and nationally (in this respect, the close liaison with local police is invaluable and offers the best available up-to-date information);
3 the extent of the risk to staff and the implications of conducting or not conducting an evacuation.

4.5.4 Evacuation

In the event of an actual major fire, bomb detonation or other incident taking place, staff will evacuate the affected premises instantly. There may be incidences of smoke inhalation, shock, various degrees of injury, loss of property, considerable trauma, disorientation and the need to cope with the loss of colleagues or friends. Even staff arriving at their place of work to find it devastated will suffer various levels of shock, trauma and bewilderment.

Staff evacuating a building should, as far as time permits, remove their personal property and take it with them because exclusion periods from premises can be considerable and staff who are unable to pick up coats, handbags, money or means to get home would effectively be stranded at the assembly point until alternative arrangements are made. Such losses would of course be permanent if an actual explosion or fire were to occur.

4.5.5 Staff assembly points

In the case of a fire or other incident that requires staff evacuation, each premises should have an initial staff assembly point which is close enough to be reached quickly for the initial roll call, while offering protection from the incident effects. In a terrorist situation,* escalation of a fire or other incident where exclusion is likely to be for an extended period, a secondary assembly point will be required which is far enough away from the devastated site to be safe and unaffected by extended cordons imposed by emergency services. The locations of these sites must be known to all members of staff.

Staff may be taken from the initial assembly point to a more protected 'secondary' assembly point by the fire wardens if circumstances dictate. This will provide a place to wait while the all-important roll-call and location of lost staff is made and a long-term, safe environment for all staff where refreshments, communication and toilet facilities is made available. It will also provide staff with increased protection from possible secondary terrorist targets and a temporary home for those in shock or who have lost coats, wallets or keys, and therefore their means of travelling to their homes. Facilities should be made available for staff who may need to be accommodated overnight or where initial trauma counselling needs to be carried out. The human resources (HR) department may need to provide cash or other facilities in order that some staff can make their way home while others regroup prior to initiating business restart procedures at alternative sites.

All emergency services vehicles would normally be parked between the two cordons during an incident. While civilian entry may be possible into the outer cordoned area relatively quickly following an incident, the inner cordoned area would be severely restricted for some considerable time, until it was considered safe to shrink it progressively. The level of safety may relate to secondary terrorist devices, dangerous buildings or falling glass. The exclusion for extended periods from premises, data, records and other facilities essential to business operations is likely to cause considerable business disruption.

Emergency staff assembly points and business continuity management control facilities must be established outside any potential cordoned areas. The scale of the potential disruption to public rights of way and transport services should be borne in mind when staff leave the assembly point to travel home or to alternative worksites.

---

*In the event of a terrorist situation, police would cordon off an exclusion zone designed to protect the public from blast, or percussive effects. The cordoned area would not be circular and would follow convenient roads and intersections. Unless the situation dictated otherwise, the inner and outer cordons could extend up to 400 and 600 yards in diameter, respectively. A similar situation could develop should a fire spread significantly or a large gas leak occur.

4.6 ACTION TO BE TAKEN UPON RECEIPT OF A THREAT CALL

There are three possible choices: (i) to evacuate staff then search the premises; (ii) to search without evacuation, and (iii) to take limited action.

4.6.1 To evacuate staff to the assembly point (and search before re-entry)

This is the most common action.

4.6.1.1 Evacuation and continuation of business elsewhere

When evacuation takes place, all business functionality may be disrupted for as little as a few hours but, if an explosion, fire or other major incident has or is about to occur, an alternative business continuity site will need to be activated without delay. The question of whether to wait or whether to invoke the business continuity plan at the alternative site is not easy to answer unless the scale of the incident is immediately obvious. However, in other than clear-cut circumstances some prior liaison with fire or police officers can provide an advisory contact which may help tip the balance of what is largely a calculated guess decision. The departmental business continuity plans, including all aspects of recovery from the point of evacuation and site destruction, are detailed in Part 2 of this book. *It must be the responsibility of departmental management to ensure that their plans and procedures are comprehensive, up to date, effective and that all staff know their emergency roles.*

4.6.1.2 Safety of important items

Staff may be asked, at the time of evacuation and while picking up their personal possessions, to shut a drawer or take a small item of importance with them on behalf of the company, such as a computer day disk, *if this does not cause delay to their exit.* Unless a bomb is very near, blast from outside is unlikely to severely damage documentation in safes, filing cabinets and so on, BUT it is likely to suck all loose paper through shattered windows and deposit it over a wide area. As a general policy, therefore, loose paperwork, of an important nature, should not be left out on desks, and a 'clear desk' policy should become part of daily corporate housekeeping. Computer disks are fragile but if all information is regularly backed up to a central networked processor, *located at a remote site*, loss of information should be minimal and system reinstatement at the BC alternative site (known as a 'hot start site') should be rapid.

4.6.1.3 Search (within a premises)

1 After premises have been evacuated and the time limit for a threatened event has elapsed, a reasonable margin of time should be allowed before selected volunteers re-enter the premises to search for any suspect item (Appendix 5). A search should only be made following consultation with police and in any event both police and fire services should be informed of what is to be undertaken.
2 The responsibility for searching private premises lies with the company – NOT with the police or other emergency services. Although police may offer to assist with searches, they will obviously be unfamiliar with either the building or its likely contents.
3 Bearing in mind the multiplicity of form which a bomb can take, as well as

its disguised packaging, it is the unusual object anywhere, or a familiar object not in its normal place, which would be suspect. Once again, only the company staff with local area knowledge, such as section fire wardens, would be in a realistic position to search and assess quickly and effectively. There is obviously a need for inter-occupier liaison where the problem is exacerbated by multi-tenanted properties that have areas common to various occupiers.

4 Searching should be on a predetermined and methodical grid-base system and those areas, searched by departmental volunteers (Appendix 5), must be covered comprehensively. The search co-ordinator should verify secured areas and retain lists completed by the searchers to ensure a double check (Appendix 6). Where areas are secured, they may be sealed with tags or locked as necessary.

5 Suspect objects should not be interfered with and when found, police should be informed immediately by the search co-ordinator or BC administrator. Portable radio transmitters or mobile telephones must not be used near suspect items.

6 Searchers are volunteer staff members. By the very nature of their normal job, security and property administration departments frequently make up the bulk of such volunteers. However, at least one person from each department is required to act as 'spotter' for unusual or out-of-place items within their familiar work environment. Assistance to search from members of the public or contractors should NEVER be accepted. Departmental 'spotters' should be included with listed searchers and both groups must be trained at regular intervals.

4.6.2 To search without external evacuation

(Moving staff to a safe 'core' of the building)

This is not common practice but it can, in certain circumstances, have considerable merit.

4.6.2.1 Remaining within the building

If it is believed that a bomb or other potential danger is likely to be outside the immediate fabric of the building, such as in the street, a vehicle or another building, it may be safer for staff to remain within the protection of their own building. Bringing them toward the inner core, or basement areas, and away from windows or areas likely to be penetrated by blast can offer considerable levels of protection. The alternative, that of external evacuation, may simply drive staff out on to the streets and into the path of a hidden explosive device which could be detonated by remote control; the perpetrators expecting just such a reaction.

The decision to 'evacuate internally' should only be made upon police advice following assessment of the situation and a full search of the premises which comprises the 'protective envelope'. It should be borne in mind that not all premises are suitable for 'internal' evacuation, and if this is considered an option a prior structural survey should be conducted to determine suitability.

4.6.3 To take limited action

Limited action might be appropriate when a terrorist threat appears to be a hoax. Where information is of unknown validity and the overwhelming weight of evidence suggests a hoax call, then a decision not to evacuate could be justified. While it is still necessary to conduct a limited search, and make a positive decision concerning evacuation, the following pre-planning would make such a decision easier:

1 Full documentation concerning the number of areas that need to be searched and how quickly and thoroughly this can be achieved. Such areas may, however, be extensive or of shared occupancy and include entrances, post rooms, storage rooms, garages, parked cars, toilets and communication areas.
2 The practice of pre-searching and sealing areas, to ensure safety zones which do not need searching again. Electrical switching rooms, archives, storage rooms, risers and ducting are frequently excluded from further search in this way.

The apparent lack of reaction to a hoax call (that is, mass evacuation), may well deter such callers from further attempts. The object is frequently to see whether their calls can elicit the spectacle of workers leaving their places, and a positive reaction in this way to repeated calls is likely to perpetuate the hoax.

It is essential that police are consulted before plans involving non-evacuation are implemented

4.7 DEVICE DETONATION

4.7.1 Detonation of a device prior to, or during, evacuation

In the event of an explosion without prior warning or during an evacuation or search, the situation will be actioned as any other major incident, including a fire. There may be more than one device and it may be safer to remain rather than flee the building. Depending on whether the explosion started a fire or seriously damaged the fabric of the building, the senior person in attendance must decide, on balance, whether it is safer to remain or evacuate. In any event the police and emergency services will quickly take charge of the situation and evacuate staff via a pre-cleared safety route. Anyone already in the process of evacuation to their assembly point must not return to help their work colleagues.

4.7.1.1 Location of utilities and heavy objects

The property services manager should be responsible for liaison with police and emergency services concerning the location of electricity, gas and water supplies, together with the location of any above-ground heavy objects, such as machinery, fireproof filing cabinets or safes which may fall through weakened floors. Site plans must be readily available, copies of which should be lodged with local fire authorities and updated where necessary.

4.7.1.2 Location of staff

Human resources (HR) management should liaise with police at the time of a major incident in order to constantly update a list which identifies staff locations as well as those members of staff who are injured, trapped or missing. This reinforces the need for discipline at assembly points and the greatest co-operation in completing roll calls. The police will take responsibility for notifying the victims' next of kin and relatives of casualties. Information for relatives of those likely to be late home as well as all related incoming enquiries from family or the public will be the responsibility of the HR department.

4.7.2 Letter bombs or incendiary devices

Both have seen only sporadic use on the UK mainland. The former saw extensive use on the Irish mainland as part of an IRA random targeting policy while the latter have been used by hard-line animal rights organizations against the retail environment.

4.7.2.1 What is a letter bomb or incendiary device?

A suspect letter bomb is any parcel, package or letter delivered through the post or private delivery service which may contain an explosive charge and is likely to detonate on opening. Incendiary devices may be very small and may be hand delivered in some way by the maker. They are frequently detonated by a chemical timer and are imprecise. Because of the small amount of 'fuel' available in a very small package, they are frequently put inside combustible display goods or office papers and used just as an initiator.

4.7.2.2 Recognizing a device

Small explosive and incendiary devices can take many forms but they are almost never large. Considerable problems can arise in identifying them because they can be so easily camouflaged. Explosive devices can be disguised to appear as packaged office items, sound or video cassettes, or free samples. An incendiary device could be as small as a packet of ten cigarettes.

Most letter bomb devices are sent through the Royal Mail and company post room staff must take care when receiving any packages which are unusually lumpy, heavy or unbalanced for their size.

Other suspicious packaging points to note are:

- wires or electronic components spread out in an envelope
- greasy or sweaty marks on the envelope perhaps making the ink run
- an 'odd-looking' name and address or unusual writing or style of address
- a 'chemical' smell, perhaps of almonds or marzipan
- unusual wrapping (that is, with lots of adhesive tape)
- no clear postmark
- unusual foreign postmarks
- the appearance of containing a book-shaped item that is unexpected, rattles or is unusually light or heavy
- an unusual number or value of stamps
- a rigid or semi-rigid envelope.

Any suspicion concerning a possible device should be reported to senior management and this may be by notifying the switchboard staff, who would pass the warning via the emergency reporting telephone system as already discussed. No immediate attempt should be made to move the suspect item and the close vicinity should be vacated by ALL staff.

4.7.2.3 Handling

It must be accepted that any device which has withstood the rigorous handling encountered during the course of postal transit can, with care, be moved in safety within the premises to a place where it can be temporarily stored – PROVIDED there has been no attempt to open it. However, this should only be undertaken if essential and only by a designated person (Appendix 7).

Since explosive devices which have been delivered by post are designed to activate when opened, they can be examined externally in reasonable safety provided that:

• the package is not damaged
• it is done carefully and without the use of, or near, metal or electromagnetic devices
• no attempt is made to open it
• it is not subject to blows, crushing, bending or being dropped
• it is not immersed in water.

4.7.2.4 If in doubt

In cases of doubt, an initial attempt to check the origin of the letter or package should be made. Post room staff may, for example, be able to suggest possible names of senders from the style of packing and a telephone call may immediately resolve the problem, or a check with staff may produce an acknowledgement that the package is expected.

4.7.2.5 Informing the police

In the event that the above action does not produce results, the letter/package should be placed in a safe, dry, non-flammable environment, which is not accessible to staff, subject to radio transmissions or electromagnetic radiation (generators, electrical plant rooms and so on). Police should be informed.

4.8 ALTERNATIVE SITES OF OPERATION

In the event of serious damage to, or exclusion from, key premises all businesses would have an urgent need for specific, predetermined alternative site facilities in order to establish continuity of critical business functionality, even in a reduced form. These, together with re-established computer systems and back-up data are likely to be required within one working day to ensure adequate continuity.

4.8.1 Continuity of business services

This is detailed in Part 2 of this book, and is subdivided on the basis of time-prioritized departmental facility needs. It is obviously not possible to include every combination of facility requirements for every business and this plan is based on the typical needs of the financial industry with realistic timescales:

• Computer access to be available within three hours of a major incident taking place.
• Electronic information facilities also to be available within three hours.
• Office space and normal office equipment, including PCs to be available for

'key' staff within three hours and expanding to agreed levels within 24 hours (see departmental sheets in Part 2 of this book).

- Reduced office facilities to be available within the same working day and to a full pre-incident level within 21 days.
- The recovery of working records from IT back-up files within one working day and immediately accessible ideally, data back-up at a remote site, on a 'live-time' basis. Should this not be the case, an analysis should be undertaken of the potential quantity and importance of data that may be lost. If, for example, business information is backed up on a once-a-day basis, a company must be prepared to lose data for a complete day if its primary IT is destroyed just prior to back-up. If this is not satisfactory, working practices or IT equipment must be changed to accommodate the level of back-up required.
- The availability of all critical hard copy documentation (outstanding invoices, tax records and so on) within one working week. If these documents are not duplicated in hard copy or stored offsite, it may be necessary to provide an electronic copy and storage facility which will interface with the IT system and therefore be available to relevant departments at alternative sites of operation.

NB Salvage of lost information, equipment and documentation forms Part 3 of this book.

Protection of company records and general documentation

5.1 PREMISES

5.1.1 Explosion within or nearby company premises

A bomb outside the premises or an explosion inside the premises, which was not large enough to cause structural collapse, would have the following effects:

- All windows would be blown either outwards or inwards.
- Anything likely to suffer from percussive pressure, such as PC screens, would implode.
- All loose documentation not in metal cabinets could be sucked out or blown out by blast and scattered over large public area.
- Loose papers could cause a number of small fires which may spread.
- Wooden desks, chairs and soft furnishings may be shredded by the blast and add fuel to any fire.

A Bomb blast, except in extreme cases, would be unlikely to collapse the building structure and the majority of properly stored documents would remain intact although not necessarily accessible.

Following a serious event, each piece of paper which is found without a file cover or other means of identification, partly burnt, sodden or filthy, may well be the one piece of great importance. In addition, there is a loss of client information confidentiality if paperwork should be sucked from broken windows by blast and deposited over a wide area of the local streets. At the very least, it is likely to consume considerable employee time in collecting such items and deciding whether they should be retained, cleaned, dried and filed, rather than scrapped. This use of staff time when it can least be spared, together with the loss of information, will be a direct result of inappropriate document storage and will severely hamper the process of returning to normal functionality.

Despite the idea of the paperless office, most businesses still currently store large quantities of paper, and there is a need to substantially improve document management, including archives. A seriously damaged building could be off limits for some time and the inability to reach documentation known to be intact, could render it 'unusable'.

5.2 PROTECTION OF RECORDS

5.2.1 Preservation methods

There are three main ways of preserving records or documentation:

- storage on a corporate networked computer system and backed up at another location
- the protection of existing documentation at present in hard copy form with off-site storage of duplicates either in hard copy or electronic form
- removal to a safer site and storage of essential hard copy while either duplicates in hard copy or electronic form are used for daily working purposes.

The second and third points may also depend upon the value or legal requirement to retain the original document.

5.2.1.1 Storage on the corporate network computer system

It is now common practice for networked business PC server systems to be used for the storage of commonly accessed data. This allows original documentation to be safely archived offsite, while giving instant PC access for daily use. Networked systems are typically backed up offsite (that is, copied electronically to a different location) throughout the day in live time, but older and slower systems, as well as those with insufficient transmission capacity, may only be capable of back-up every 24 hours, usually during the night when the network is quiet. In the event of a major incident involving severe damage to a business site, data would be available at alternative corporate sites or at the designated BC back-up site. However, for those systems which are slow, as discussed, and where back-up to an offsite location requires an extended period, it is possible for considerable data to be lost if a disaster event occurs just prior to back-up.

5.2.1.2 The protection of existing documentation currently stored as hard copy

It is probably not possible to totally protect bulk paperwork from flood, fire or explosive damage in both a cost effective and easily accessible manner. Consideration must therefore be given to the following alternatives:

- As far as possible replace hard copy in a more convenient form.
- Duplicate and store offsite.

However, all documentation must be reviewed and managed against the parameters of legal requirement, criticality and redundancy:

- retention and protection as a legal requirement
- retention because contained information is of a critical or sensitive nature and the company may not wish it to be stored on a computer system
- retention is useful for a limited period but not critical to departmental functionality

- retention is not critical and either the information becomes rapidly redundant or is available on other data networks.

In view of the high consumption of computer memory that results from scanning documents, it may be decided not to store hard copy documents on the business PC system, and a stand-alone system may be preferred. There are a number of such systems available which fall within the term 'business imaging and management systems' and which store the scanned information on compact discs (CD), some of which can be overwritten many times while others can only be written to only once. The advantage of the latter format is that they are intended to be acceptable in a court of law as an 'unalterable copy of an original document' as has microfiche for many years. However, to date there is no definitive ruling on the legal acceptance of CD copies for use in court.

There is frequently a considerable time delay in establishing such an electronic system throughout a company and the installation, training and discipline of use impose a considerable cost. However, there is need for adequate protection in the interim period, and it is critical that a clear-desk policy be maintained and suitable storage be used for loose box files and folders and so on.

5.2.1.3 Removal of essential hard copy documentation to a safe site

Documentation that must be retained for legal purposes should be copied and the copy used as the working document while the originals are stored in suitable vaults.

5.3 MAJOR DOCUMENTATION RETRIEVAL

Proper storage protects documentation and saves the cost of retrieval, transportation, large processing areas and extensive staff time dedicated to sorting, washing, drying, copying and filing, as well as obtaining certified duplicates where necessary. Should a major incident occur, prevention can be much cheaper than retrieval.

However, since much documentation is reduced by means of electronic filing or computer storage there will always be a quantity of paperwork which remains and which will need salvaging from a devastated site. Disasters destroy documentation in various ways.

5.3.1 Explosives

Explosives shred paperwork and can blast it from windows. Scattered fires can occur as can mixing of filing systems.

5.3.2 Fire

Fire burns or chars documents, making them brittle and soot-stained. With special treatment most burnt documents are retrievable but plastic file covers, when melted into documents, frequently makes them irretrievable.

5.3.3 Water

Water, under pressure, bursts open cardboard files, scatters and soaks paperwork. Sodden files quickly grow mould, stick together and pulp. Drain-away water causes similar problems but carries dirt, soot, sewage and other water transportable effluent.

5.4 ARCHIVAL STORAGE

5.4.1 Free-standing document safes and fireproof data storage cabinets

In the event of a severe fire or explosion any free-standing safes, fireproof storage cabinets or high-density storage systems, above ground level, are in danger of falling through a weakened or collapsing floor slab. While it is likely that safes alone would retain their integrity in such circumstances, most other storage media are likely to be extensively damaged and fail to protect contents.

5.4.2 Recovery potential

Whether safe storage units fall through floors or not, it is unlikely that they could be retrieved until building safety was ensured and this may be weeks rather than days following an incident. It is also unlikely that, once subject to blast or severe fire, they could not be opened onsite and may require transfer to a safer, cleaner and drier environment before being opened by safe engineers. As far as possible therefore, all valuable documentation should be safeguarded as discussed and stored in a place which would not be subject to a common damage.

5.5 CORPORATE HEADQUARTERS

5.5.1 Vault storage

Many corporate headquarters, particularly those that have been established for many years, retain some form of high-security basement storage, which may generally be termed 'vaults'. Documents of incorporation, works of art, client deeds, patents and a whole variety of valuable items may be stored in them since they are not part of the daily business process. While vaults do offer extremely high levels of protection it must be noted that it is possible to envisage a situation where access to them could be delayed for very extended periods, if the site could not be accessed on safety grounds. The vault units are likely to protect their contents even if the building totally collapsed or was destroyed by fire, but contrary to popular belief they do not necessarily offer protection against water ingress. Vault access could be delayed by the need to clear and shore up an access path and pump out the accumulation of water used to extinguish a fire.

NB Offers by the fire brigade to pump out basements are not uncommon immediately following an incident but such offers should be declined. Fire brigade pumps operate at a very high pressure and will pulp any floating documentation.

Section 6

Staff

6.1 STAFF PROTECTION, REHOUSING AND TRAINING

6.1.1 Staff awareness of duties

It is most important that staff are made aware of what is required of them, both in terms of self-preservation and their duty to others in their charge following a major incident. The following four points are considered to be critical and should be addressed effectively:

- The rapid evacuation of staff to a place of safety and not just into the street.
- The disadvantage of roll-call procedures which may be undertaken in the street with the possibility of inclement weather, exposure to further incident repercussions or terrorist activity.
- Instructions and alternative facilities for assembled staff, should they not be able to return to their place of work within a designated time or because of public or traffic congestion resulting from terrorist or other incidents.
- The need to contact staff quickly should an incident occur outside normal working hours.

6.1.2 Key staff

Depending on the number of corporate sites available, it may be impractical to accommodate staff from an evacuated site at other operational sites, and attempts to do so may further interrupt work schedules, cause delays and produce employee friction. In the short term, unless there is adequate space available, it is a working rule that all but key personnel from an abandoned site should be sent home.

Within the first few hours following an event, key staff should have pre-allocated alternative working locations to begin restart procedures immediately, but during this initial period they are unlikely to exceed 20–25 per cent of the original site staff. It is important to control the numbers of staff in order to prevent unneeded but willing crowds clogging the restart site. Other staff should be progressively absorbed into the business continuity site, existing sites, or into rented office space over a period of time.

Part 2 of this book contains broad sample details of: (a) staff relocations, (b) staff duties and (c) the staffing levels during the first 20 days following a major incident. It is imperative that staffing, facilities and accommodation levels are agreed with senior BC management and that departmental management inform

BC administration of any changes they require to staffing or equipment levels, or timescales.

6.1.3 Staff training (safety)

The HR department is normally responsible for staff training and the many practical problems involving staff at times of major incident. Experience of disaster situations has revealed the following to be typical problems:

- Staff do not know the location or cannot get to the roll-call assembly point.
- Police intervention prevents assembly at the proposed location or fails to provide a route to a secondary location.
- Staff are without coats/handbags and so on and therefore have no means of returning home.
- Staff are in a state of shock and therefore in need of rest facilities.
- The lack of available staff records giving telephone numbers, next of kin, whether present or away from work, location of work area and so on may prevent essential contact.
- The lack of staff trained in trauma counselling who may be needed to give 'first aid' in shock situations.
- The lack of skills in the broader duties of both fire wardens covering evacuation and roll-call, and first aid staff caring for those who are distressed rather than injured.

In the interests of staff welfare there is a need to develop personnel related aspects of the BC plan and short courses made available to fill these gaps.

6.1.4 Staff training (business functionality)

Business departments frequently express the opinion that their own working systems are unique and would only be operational if experienced staff were available. If this is indeed true, the availability of staff with key operating, broad-based skills, who can function with severely reduced ancillary staffing levels, is a critical factor for rapid business restart following an incident.

The resolution of this problem is to be found in a programme of critical area cross-training of key personnel and the detailed documentation of departmental operating instructions in major incident circumstances. There are frequently a number of closely related departments where cross-training on systems would be practical and highly cost effective, but this relies on effective co-operation between departments and the breaking down of protectionist barriers. Normal working practices, while proving most efficient when all key staff are available, may prove a disadvantage should a major incident prevent these persons from attending their place of work while others are insufficiently trained to 'hold the fort'.

In order to facilitate easier cross-training, detailed BC procedures should be maintained and updated by each department. The HR department may liaise with departmental heads to identify the cross-training needs and instigate suitable programmes as follows:

- broader training so that key staff can operate in more than one department
- more inter-departmental staff training in emergency, fire and first aid procedures

- full training for all staff in what would be expected of them should a major incident occur
- departmental operating instructions for use in emergency situations.

6.2 FIRE WARDENS

Corporate fire wardens, with additional training in emergency evacuation and roll-call procedures, would be the logical choice for staff control duties at times of major incident.

6.2.1 Training

While training should still include normal fire fighting methods, broader training could also cover those skills needed subsequent to the fire brigade or police leaving the site, when recovery becomes the responsibility of staff. Training may include the following:

- control and evaluation of the damaged site
- business continuity management
- use of specialist advisors.

6.2.2 Suitability of staff

The HR department may need to ensure that staff who wish to volunteer for major incident training are suited to such tasks as this may well include involvement with seriously injured persons who are also colleagues. HR will also need to ensure that suitable staff have enough time from their normal duties to undertake emergency role training, and that the movement of trained staff due to transfer, promotion or natural wastage is monitored and that they are replaced where necessary.

6.2.3 Property services or facilities management department

The majority of businesses employ or contract a contingent of 'front line' staff in the form of the property services or facilities management department. Their detailed knowledge of the premises, together with their electrical, plumbing and building skills, render them invaluable in both planning for, and recovery from, major incidents. In time of such events this department should be closely involved with the BC committee and be included on major incident training courses.

6.3 ADDITIONAL STAFF

The timescale of recovery from a major incident situation will be dramatically affected by staff availability to carry out normal business functions, but there may be a considerable unexpected short-fall of availability if, for the following reasons, staff are:

- physically injured or mentally traumatized

- unable to get to or function effectively at the emergency site
- used to set up emergency facilities
- used at relocation host sites prior to services reinstatement
- used at emergency control points
- involved with salvage operations
- used to cope with the considerable increase in telephone traffic, reassure clients, and compensate for the extra time needed to operate unfamiliar, smaller, or manual switchboard systems.

As a result, there is likely to be a requirement for an *increase* in temporary staff with good basic office skills. An average figure for a major incident site which is mainly office orientated would be: an additional 20 per cent of existing staff for the first week; an additional 10 per cent for the following four weeks; and 5 per cent for a further 12 weeks. Requirements for additional temporary staff should be co-ordinated by the HR management in consultation with the BC administration and departmental management.

Business continuity representatives

7.1 BUSINESS CONTINUITY (BC) PLAN

As discussed briefly in the introduction, a business continuity plan is a series of smaller plans designed to integrate all aspects of corporate operations. Each department is responsible for the documentary compilation and update of its own procedures and requirements, ensuring that all aspects of inter-departmental recovery are integrated where necessary and essential functionality is maintained.

BC representatives are responsible, in consultation with the appointed BC administration and management, for formulating the overall departmental plans within the following parameters:

- Writing procedures and checklists of things to do, in the event of a major incident, at each departmental level.
- Addressing the various needs likely to result from different types and severity of incident, and loss of staff.
- Documenting detailed requirements for equipment, stationery, furniture and services required for satisfactory functionality.
- Establishing housekeeping procedures such as updating staff call-out lists and telephone numbers.
- Establishing 'on-call' emergency staff procedures, mobile communications facilities and the provision of staff call-out priority lists (known as 'cascade lists').
- Determining staff relocation requirements such a numbers of desks, PCs, types of software, or specialized facilities.
- Establishing chains of communications, responsibility and authority with BC management.
- Detailing staff duties, rotas, responsibilities and time frames for their mobilization.

In order to become familiar with all the concerned procedures, each department should formulate its own plan within the boundary of the overall plan. The degree of detail provided should enable individuals, separately tasked within the department, to fulfil a predetermined level of business functionality.

7.2 REGULAR BC MEETINGS

It is essential that 'core' service departments and those representing BC administration and management meet regularly while all other departments have representatives who can attend when a meeting is pertinent to their particular departmental needs.

7.2.1 Key responsibilities of BC representatives

Although BC representatives are volunteers, they will be expected to undertake a key role in continuity planning, instructing their own departments and assuming a facilitating role at the BC site should a major incident occur. Those who have a key role in actual business recovery at the time of an incident, such as computer technicians, would not be readily available to assist with the wider aspects of recovery management, and therefore should not be used as BC representatives. However, such departments do need some level of BC training in order to understand the overall planning strategy and integrate their own recovery plans, priorities and timescales.

7.2.2 Core department representatives at BC meetings

Core department representatives essential for participating in, or giving advice to, the BC committee are:

- senior management (usually as chairman)
- appointed business recovery administrator(s)
- property services (facilities) management
- security
- health and safety
- telecommunications
- computer (IT)
- internal audit (financial sector only)
- personnel (HR) and training
- commercial division (sales)
- manufacturing
- public relations and marketing
- records (archives)
- other departments, depending on the business concerned.

7.3 DOCUMENTATION RESULTING FROM MEETINGS

Each departmental representative should have a personal copy of the BC plan and be expected to notify the BC administrator of any aspects requiring modification, addition, deletion or update. Once alterations are agreed and made, specific revised BC instruction sheet(s) should be sent to each representative for inclusion in departmental copies of the plan. All changes or modifications to the BC plan that are significant and materially affect members of staff can be circulated, with explanatory notes, via a staff information bulletin sheet.

7.4 BC ADMINISTRATION DUTY ROTA

It is important that, should a major incident develop, there is the ability for a designated number of BC management and administration staff to be at the site quickly, irrespective of the time or day. All such staff may therefore be classified according to their ability to attend quickly. Those who can attend within an acceptable timescale, as defined by senior management but normally within one hour, can be included on an 'immediate call-out' duty rota and form the initial response group. Their role would be to make a rapid assessment of the required response and take responsibility for initiating emergency procedures, invocation of emergency sites and calling out other members of staff as thought necessary.

7.5 EMERGENCY SUPPLIERS

The BC administrator, in liaison with facilities management, should collate sufficient information concerning the availability of private emergency services, builders, salvage companies and suppliers of any facility that may be required in an emergency situation. It is essential that such lists are regularly updated and included in the BC manual for staff reference.

7.6 SPECIALIST ADVISORS

It should not be possible for a major incident to occur which has not already been considered, at least in terms of its effect, and a suitable contingency plan established. However, such unforeseen events do occur and the BC management may require specialist advice. A telephone directory should give extensive reference contact numbers and addresses of specialists such as structural engineers, aviation engineers, the meteorological office, forensic fire experts and media consultants. It is again essential that this be regularly updated.

Incident control point

8.1 INCIDENT MANAGEMENT CONTROL POINT

The incident management control point (IMCP) is a fully equipped office facility and is frequently sited within the emergency BC site. It serves a multiple role, being the centre for BC management throughout the period the business operates at the emergency site and being a convenient place for meetings with insurers, builders and others associated with the damaged site. A secondary IMCP, in the form of a mobile or portable building, is often located near to the damaged site, in order that site security and salvage procedures can be put in place and corporate representatives can meet with builders.

8.1.1 Human resources management of those missing or injured

At the time of a major incident, the HR department will make the following information available to the IMCP staff. They will also liaise with emergency services in order to ensure that the fullest and most up-to-date information concerning those missing or injured is always available to relatives and medical staff:

- a photograph (for identification purposes)
- home address
- next of kin (with first name)
- home telephone number
- any other telephone or pager numbers
- blood group and allergies.

8.1.2 Street plans

Plans of the streets surrounding the affected corporate premises should be held by staff at the IMCP because a major incident can cause severe congestion to road systems within a large area. If the incident involves suspected explosives, secondary devices, extensive fire spread, flooded or blacked out (without electrical power) areas, emergency services may cordon off extensive areas and the simple matter of getting staff home may require walking to unfamiliar locations.

8.1.3 Mobile telephones

The likely need for staff to meet with engineers and contractors at, or close to, the damaged site, and be in contact with the IMCP, dictates that mobile telephones must be available. Communications departments must be kept informed of likely requirements or an emergency requirement contract can be established with mobile telephone suppliers. It is important that there are ample battery chargers and spare batteries available.

8.1.4 Premises layout

Detailed floor plans of all business premises, showing service layouts including air conditioning ducting, electrical supplies and consumer units, gas and water supply stop cocks and sprinkler systems, will be held by the property services (facilities) manager at the IMCP, for use by emergency services. Fire brigades welcome information concerning heavy items, such as safes, which are above ground level and could fall through weakened floors. This could save firemen from being crushed should a floor carrying such an item suddenly collapse. Concrete floor slabs are not immune from collapse when subject to extreme heat.

8.1.5 High-worth property

If the incident is a fire or flood, the fire brigade may be asked to secure high-worth property, if they are able to do so, before it is destroyed. High-value paintings come into this category and their locations should therefore be noted on floor plans.

8.1.6 Water riser pipes and valves

The fire brigade will require information concerning water riser pipes and valves, whether they are 'dry' or 'wet', the position of them and their floor outlets, in order that fire fighting equipment can be connected. Plans should be suitably marked and supplied to emergency services.

8.1.7 Control point protocol

8.1.7.1 Use of action and status wall charts

In order that staff working different shifts at the IMCP do not duplicate effort and become involved with a single incident or problem, on-going matters should be noted on an action and status wall chart.

Status lists may also include the following:

- computer facilities available (with time based update)
- computer facilities likely to be available (with estimated go live time)
- manufacturing capacity
- stock availability
- progress of business reinstatement
- any list which indicates the progressive status of a return to business functionality.

An 0800 (freephone) telephone call-in system can be very useful in providing senior management and other BC staff with current status reports. Staff generally can also use the facility to update themselves on matters such as whether they are required to return to work and where they should report.

8.2 EQUIPMENT FOR USE AT THE INCIDENT SITE

8.2.1 Identification and badges

Property facilities staff are likely to be the first company representatives to re-enter an evacuated site following a major incident, in order to assess the situation and commence reclamation. It is likely that initially the emergency services or police will be in attendance and it will be necessary for:

- staff members at the site to have current identification passes or badges
- the local police to be supplied with a list of 'key persons' prior to a major incident*
- a supply of passes to be available for contractors who are authorized by the company to attend the site.
- an effective access control and identification system to be established to prevent looting from damaged sites. It is likely that this duty will be passed to a contracted guarding service once emergency and police services release the site.

Once this has taken place, the pass system will need to be extended to accommodate:

- further staff who attend the site and will need to be identified by guarding service staff
- staff who attend the premises of third party contractors for the purposes of identifying materials prior to reclamation
- staff who work at commercially contracted BC office sites
- temporary or contract staff and other visitors.

Experience has shown that the failure to have an effective pass system can cause considerable friction and delay.

8.2.2 Protective equipment

As progressively more members of staff become involved with the damaged site, the sorting and filing of documentation, or the reclamation of equipment, a need will develop for a supply of both basic protective clothing and storage containers. It is an advantage to establish a contract with a supplier prior to an incident taking place.

8.2.3 First aid equipment

First aid equipment and the services of staff who are trained in first aid will be made available by the health and safety officer at all sites where staff are employed.

*While this system is not operated by all police forces, passes and 'key persons' lists can save considerable delay in site re-entry if they are readily available.

8.2.4 Other equipment

Only designated staff should be allowed to enter dirty or damaged areas (once declared safe), or to handle contaminated objects or documentation and they must be equipped with appropriate protective clothing. Other emergency equipment should be available to the property facilities department and may typically include:

- torches
- wellington boots
- helmets
- industrial gloves
- buckets
- spades
- brooms
- plastic sheeting
- plastic bags
- a water pump
- a small portable emergency generator and lighting set
- a comprehensive tool kit.

8.3 EMERGENCY CONTRACTORS

Information concerning emergency contractors, such as structural engineers, boarding-up specialists, glaziers, hoarding and scaffolding erectors, plumbers, electricians, alarm engineers, plant hire suppliers, specialist storage or warehousing suppliers, removers, telecommunications, electricity, gas and water suppliers, rubbish removal, the emergency services, computer reclamation and document reclamation specialists, as well as all those supplying specialist services which may be required by individual businesses, must be collated and maintained as a directory within the body of the BC plan. This will need to be constantly updated and periodic contact made with preferred suppliers to ensure they are still in business.

Section 9

Continuity of management

9.1 SENIOR MANAGEMENT AND KEY STAFF WHEREABOUTS

It is essential that a member of senior management, authorized to make major policy decisions in an emergency situation, is in telephone contact at all times.

Levels of criticality at the time of an incident will also require the ability to immediately contact members of the BC administration, the property facilities department and those staff of the computer department involved with IT reinstatement.

The BC administrator should ensure that current addresses and contact telephone numbers of all senior management and other key staff are available and updated as necessary.

9.2 THE INCIDENT MANAGEMENT CONTROL POINT (IMCP) STAFF

The BC administrator manages the running of the IMCP. Varying degrees of authority are exercised by the control staff for the daily running of business continuity and recovery but the senior management on-call system enables executive involvement when required. Experience has shown that it is important to define individual specializations and responsibilities. Involvement of senior executives with limited knowledge of operating or business continuity practices should be avoided if possible.

9.2.1 Key personnel

It is to be expected that a number of key personnel will either be absent, unobtainable or a casualty at the time of a typical emergency. 'Cascade' lists should be drawn up by each business department, which specify who, in the absence of a particular key person, is the next person to take control. Depending on the company structure, the same system should also apply to senior management and operational directors. Universally, the delegation of senior management authority is known as a 'succession list'. All such persons who appear, by virtue of seniority or training, on a succession list *must* always be available by phone and trained to a standard which will enable them to function in a disaster situation. It is essential that these lists are maintained and updated regularly.

9.2.2 Duties and responsibilities

The duties and responsibilities of persons on succession lists should be clearly defined within their specific business context. While being in overall responsibility, should a major event take place, they may work alongside BC management and administration who operate from the IMCP. Staff working from the IMCP will not be free to reinstate their own departments until they are no longer required at the IMCP and should therefore make arrangements for others to take this departmental role.

9.3 DELEGATION OF AUTHORITY

The actual mix of authority exercised by the IMCP staff can be critical to successful business continuity and reinstatement. Problems frequently arise when senior management attempt to administer those areas or situations about which they have little experience or skill, so defined parameters for each group must therefore be pre-established and agreed between BC staff and senior management.

Mutual aid

10.1 MUTUAL AID PLAN

As business continuity planning is expensive both to introduce and maintain, in shared occupancy situations where some duplication is inevitable, it would be sensible to operate a mutual aid plan. Common public address (PA) systems, sophisticated protection equipment or common emergency recovery procedures and training can, for example, benefit all tenants. Shared fire, emergency training procedures and drills not only save time and cost, but also induce a more cohesive system and, at least for the purposes of protecting life, should transcend corporate boundaries.

10.2 SHARED EMERGENCY EQUIPMENT

In practice, the reality of ensuring such shared procedures are practised and that shared emergency equipment is not only maintained but regularly updated to meet changing needs is frequently problematic. Fortunately, recent health and safety legislation requires businesses which occupy multi-occupancy premises to be jointly involved in safety and emergency procedures. Tenants should meet periodically, exchange contact names and emergency telephone numbers, and be able to discuss individual and mutual security and safety needs, as well as changes which may be appropriate in landlord services. Health and safety requirements and training are the responsibility of the health and safety manager, who should co-ordinate meetings with other tenants. Despite the impractical concept of maintaining corporate exclusivity and isolation in the face of a disaster, this problem is rarely satisfactorily addressed.

Data transmission and communications

11.1 THE REQUIREMENT

Communications and IT departments should ensure that computer systems have sufficient data transmission pathways for the successful reinstatement of all critical network area links, irrespective of the extent of the damage. Consideration should be given to providing all networked sites with dual transmission lines which can enable a wider scope of site interconnection as well as live back-up capacity, in the event of a site or transmission cable damage. In addition, there will be a need to establishment emergency invocation contracts for the leasing of various systems, servers and lines as well as modems and encryption units.

11.2 TELEPHONE COMMUNICATIONS AND SWITCHBOARDS

In order that a switchboard/telephone system is fully supported at the time of a major incident, immediate action is needed to transfer all calls at the exchange, from the damaged site to emergency lines and a switchboard operator. Such a comprehensive service is available from national telecommunications suppliers and guarantees that commercial premises will have a re-established telephone exchange, linked to damaged incoming lines. This will prevent callers being met with either no answer or an unobtainable number tone, and for all practical purposes callers will not be aware that their calls have been transferred.

This will give the following advantages:

1 All key staff will have a reliable communications link that remains viable irrespective of the level of damage at the parent site.
2 Calls to damaged sites can either be diverted to other sites where adequate receiving facilities are available, or to a series of private numbers as may be applicable to staff working from home.
3 Alternative BC sites should have pre-planned and pre-installed facilities for telecommunication and switchboard connections (national suppliers will not

guarantee immediate response to emergency situations without pre-planning and delays may be measured in weeks rather than days) and would therefore be able to assume switchboard control of all incoming calls. Line facilities should have greater capacity than the facilities at the lost site in order to cope with increased phone use, commercial data systems and emergency computer data transmission.

Computer systems

12.1 THE REQUIREMENT

All main business computer systems, together with other IT services, are likely to have the highest reinstatement priority. A comprehensive plan is required, agreed by senior management, which facilitates designated user access, to defined systems, with the most recent data availability, and in a defined timescale. There is a need for IT departments to document detailed flowpaths for satisfactory reinstatement procedures for services at alternative BC sites, what capacity they will have, whether there will be system restoration prioritization and in what timescale. The normal business continuity requirement is that all such procedures and equipment should be tested live, as part of an invocation exercise, at least twice each year, with additional tests carried out at times of software or hardware update.

12.2 THE RISK

Damage to IT systems and network servers at a main server site may result in loss of computer facilities at any of the sites which are connected to that network. Servers that are backed up by duplicate 'live' systems at a remote site will be able to reinstate data with minimal delay, up to the final transaction prior to the event. However, those systems which are not backed up on a live time basis, but rather on a daily or other time lagged basis, frequently at night, risk substantial data loss should an event occur just prior to back-up taking place. Data back-up tapes or other storage media will require systematic transfer to another secure site immediately following back-up completion. This frequently causes difficulties where completion may occur in the early hours of the morning, but failure to do so could result in both the original data and back-up storage being lost at the same time.

12.3 COMPUTER HARDWARE

In the event of an incident which prevents full IT availability, a contract can usually be established with a main computer hardware supplier for the immediate supply of dedicated hardware, according to an agreed schedule, at the business continuity site. PC terminals, printers, ancillary equipment and work stations which allow key staff, with the assistance of supplier in-house IT support staff, to recreate the corporate database within a specific time, frequently in the order of four hours, is the essential aim.

The following is an example of the facilities made available by an IT supplier as part of their 'hot start' package in the event of a major incident taking place:

> Within 4 hours of invocation, resulting from a major incident occurring at a corporate premises, space would be available for (xx) members of staff at the business continuity site (address). Each person would have a desk, chair, PC terminal and telephone. Also available would be a fax machine, photocopier, lockable cabinet, shredding facility, telex machine, and a meeting room with TV, video, projector and whiteboard.

However, it is incumbent upon all departments to ensure that specific IT or other facilities which are required must be specified to both IT and BC administrative departments in order that they can be included in the contractual details. There is rarely any possibility of increasing facilities at the time of a major incident.

12.3.1 IT technical support staff

Technical support staff will need to address and document such tasks as the following in order that they can be included in live BC testing scenarios (examples only):

- installing and booting systems and activating communications links
- predetermining PC keyboard mapping
- monitoring hardware and communications performance
- setting up communications links between corporate computer and user systems
- setting up communications links between corporate computer and information services
- interfacing with various support groups and telecommunications vendors

12.3.2 Emergency system testing

A contract can be established with the main computer supplier or a commercial business recovery 'hot start' site, in order that systems will be available for live testing at least two days per year. This is to ensure that equipment can be upgraded as required and that procedures work smoothly in the case of a real invocation. A 'desktop' test can also be undertaken each year by all key departments and consists of a written scenario which details a disruptive incident. Teams of departmental representatives are given time to formulate their actions in the circumstances and make a presentation to an audience of BC administration staff who will assess the likely success of their plan. The object is to ensure that staff consider each logistic step following a major incident, and how, by whom and with what facilities it is to be accomplished.

Part 2
Business Continuity

Section 13

Overview

As previously discussed, in the event of a disaster affecting the company, at any of its sites and at whatever time, a series of interlinked recovery plans should be developed to enable critical business functions to be restored within a defined timescale. It is suggested that initial recovery, at predetermined recovery sites, should be able to commence within two hours of action invocation and be complete within 12 hours. Business functionality should plan to increase to a maximum within five days and could remain in this mode for approximately 21 days. Further relocation thereafter would depend upon the period of restoration of the original site or the establishment of long-term alternative accommodation and facilities. However, commercial 'hot start' business continuity sites are frequently geared to 30-day use periods only and this is likely to impose its own timetable and discipline for further relocation.

13.1 CONTROL POINT

As discussed in Part 1, a control point (at the BC centre) should be set up immediately following the decision by management to invoke the business continuity plan. This will be staffed by members of the business continuity management team who will assume control of the recovery process and both liaise with affected departments and implement necessary decisions.

13.2 RECOVERY OF VITAL RECORDS

The recovery of vital records from the offsite storage locations would be undertaken by the respective departments and taken to the recovery site, or accessed directly from an IT retrieval storage system. Departments would be able to recover and resume operations at the locations as detailed in the departmental plan sections (see Section 24).

13.3 BUSINESS RECOVERY CENTRE

The primary business continuity centre will be at [full address, telephone number, and reference to an attached street plan]. Critical computer facilities will be resumed in accordance with the procedures contained in the computer department contingency plan and the systems will be made available via links established by the communications department.

Action to be taken in the event of a major incident

This section details procedures to be followed when a warning of an imminent incident has been received, or a major incident has taken place which is likely to seriously disrupt business functionality. Some areas duplicate those to be found in Part 1 of this plan.

14.1 EMERGENCY PROCEDURES

The action to be taken will depend upon the time of day. If warning of an imminent incident is received by any member of staff during normal business hours, that person will take the following action.

They will telephone the central switchboard and inform the operator of what information they have. The operator will then pass this information to senior management via a dedicated conference call telephone system and any one recipient can give the order to evacuate the building or take other appropriate action.

14.2 EVACUATION INFORMATION

Evacuation information must always be given centrally from the telephone switchboard using the emergency public address (PA) system, in order that all staff are informed. Once the switchboard operator has announced that evacuation is to take place, the PA can sound an evacuation chime, which must be distinct from that used to warn of fire, and will continue throughout the emergency.

Evacuation procedures

15.1 NORMAL 'FIRE' EMERGENCY EVACUATION

The normal 'fire' emergency evacuation procedures must be carried out without delay. If possible, switchboard or security staff will try to pinpoint the direction of possible danger by viewing the addressable fire alarm panel and instruct evacuation in an appropriate direction by the use of the PA system. **SWITCHBOARD OR SECURITY STAFF MUST NOT DELAY THEIR OWN EVACUATION OR PUT THEMSELVES IN DANGER**.

15.2 FIRE WARDENS

Fire wardens should carry out their normal warden duties in order to expedite evacuation whatever the cause of the emergency.

15.3 ESSENTIAL PERSONAL BELONGINGS

Staff should be trained to take their essential personal belongings with them but only if this is possible without delaying their escape or placing themselves in greater danger. They may also be asked to shut a drawer or take a small item of importance with them, such as a PC disk, if this causes no delay to their exit.

Section 16

Assembly points

16.1 PRIMARY AND SECONDARY ASSEMBLY POINTS

Each corporate premises should have a staff assembly point in the event of fire
and a further assembly point, which is much further away and within a
building, in case of a terrorist or other incident. The locations of these sites
should be listed and included in both staff handbooks and departmental BC
plans.

16.2 STAFF TO REMAIN AT ASSEMBLY POINTS

Staff should make their way to the appropriate fire assembly point, under the
guidance of the fire wardens, as quickly as possible and REMAIN THERE
until instructed to take further action – see Section 17.1.

Action at assembly points

17.1 PRIMARY ASSEMBLY POINT

While at the primary or fire assembly points, the presence of staff should be recorded by the fire wardens. Those not present at this time will be recorded as missing and will be reported to the emergency services. Staff so reported will be searched for at site by the emergency services/police and if not located will be officially reported as missing. It is essential that the roll-call procedure is taken seriously in order to avoid wasting police or fire officers' time and putting them in unnecessary danger. Staff should not disperse from the assembly point until told to do so.

17.2 DECISION TO RETURN TO WORK

In the case of a fire warning, the decision to return to work or to release staff for the day will be made quickly in order to prevent extended assembly time in a street location.

17.3 SECONDARY ASSEMBLY POINT

In the case of a bomb, other major incident or where no decision is possible for some time, the secondary assembly point would provide staff with protection within a building and with warmth, seating, refreshments, toilet facilities and telephones.

Circumstances may determine that:

- staff are unable to return to their place of work quickly because the situation remains unclear
- staff should remain at the assembly point for some time for their own safety, because they are traumatized or are awaiting collection by relatives
- staff may need to remain at the assembly point because they cannot get home for some time, or may even need to stay overnight
- key staff may need to go to an alternative worksite location as soon as possible but must wait until initial preparation is complete.

It is the responsibility of the BC management team to obtain the best available information, keep staff well informed of the situation and take decisive action.

Counselling of staff and casualties

18.1 DISTRESSED STAFF

The HR department is responsible for assisting those in a distressed or traumatized state or those unable to get home by virtue of transport disruptions, loss of personal possessions or the lateness of the hour. Counselling, transport, cash advances, calls to relatives and hotel facilities and so on. should be made readily available and each will need some level of pre-planned facility agreement.

18.2 CASUALTIES

If a major incident is such that there are, or are believed to be, casualties among staff, the BC control centre should have dedicated emergency telephone numbers staffed by HR for use by callers enquiring about the welfare of relatives or friends. These emergency numbers should be given to all staff as part of their staff employment package and updated as necessary. No outgoing calls should be made from these numbers in order to allow the best possible capacity for incoming calls. As far as possible, relatives and friends should be deterred from attending the scene.

18.2.1 Temporarily lost casualties

It is common for casualties to become temporarily 'lost' when removed by emergency services to any of a number of hospitals or first aid centres. It is the responsibility of the HR department to:

• locate those staff casualties
• notify both the BC control centre and the police, who are responsible for notifying the next of kin
• make any appropriate arrangements with family and friends.

18.2.2 Incidents outside working hours

If a major incident occurs outside normal working hours, it will be the responsibility of the HR department to determine whether any members of staff may have been onsite working late or on a shift. They will need to ensure that the emergency services are aware of who was onsite at the time of the incident, their usual location on the premises, and try to determine where they are, if taken to hospital. Liaison should be maintained with both the BC control centre and the police or other emergency services.

Section 19

Staff sent home

Staff sent home following a disaster situation and without prior arrangement for a return to work should be encouraged not to telephone the company or BC sites asking for information. Constant telephoning will quickly overload any emergency communications facilities in place and this must be avoided. All information concerning return to work or relocation details and arrangements are most conveniently dealt with by the use of an emergency free call-in number such as the '0800' system, which is available from all major telecommunications suppliers. Staff should also be contacted either by the BC administrator, their departmental BC representative or HR department who will inform them when they are to return to work. In order to retain good staff morale, it is important that staff who remain at home are given regular updates on the situation.

Management notification

20.1 NOTIFICATION OF GENERAL MANAGEMENT

Whatever the time of the incident, senior members of management and the business continuity committee MUST be notified. As previously discussed, during office hours the switchboard staff will carry out this function via an emergency conference telephone system. Staff must be aware that speed is of the essence and it is the responsibility of those obtaining the information to disseminate it as widely as possible in the best way available at the time.

20.2 MAJOR INCIDENT OUTSIDE OF BUSINESS HOURS

If a major incident occurs outside of business hours, each site will require very specific instructions for senior management notification. Should sites be without 24-hour staffing or a security presence, the provision of other notification methods and responses will be required. It is not possible to cover all eventualities by means of example, but the following gives practical instances (Sites A, B, C) that utilize alarms and other normally available services. Notification of an incident should be to designated staff who hold cascade telephone lists and are trained to react to emergency incidents and are therefore able to notify management and BC staff in the correct sequence.

20.2.1 Site A

Notification will either be by the site security guards when on duty, or by the first contract keyholder (usually a security company). These are normally informed by the intruder or fire alarm monitoring company as the result of an intruder or fire alarm activation, and consequently the emergency services will also be notified.

20.2.2 Site B

There is no appropriate out-of-business hours guard system at this site and notification of an incident is likely to be via the keyholder system as at site A. However, in addition to the use of intruder and fire alarm systems, the site can also be remotely monitored by both sound and vision (CCTV), which may increase the chances of early detection.

20.2.3 Site C

There is no manned guarding facility at this site, which is an archive store and only visited by staff when items are required. As this is essentially an unstaffed facility, security staff at site A can monitor site C by means of a CCTV system. Any incident which takes place would need to activate an intruder or fire alarm or be witnessed by security guards via the CCTV system before action could take place.

20.2.4　Responsibilities of staff with cascade phone list duties

Upon notification of an incident, those staff holding cascade phone lists should: FIRST try to clarify the nature and scope of the incident; SECOND, if the situation appeared to warrant it, call a duty business continuity committee member and inform him/her of the situation; and, THIRD, visit the affected site as quickly as possible and personally assess the likely level of response required. The information, passed to the duty BC committee member, could then be relayed to management and may be used as a basis to invoke the BC plan and assemble key staff at the BC control centre.

Damage appraisal and exclusion estimation

If either damage to a corporate site has occurred, or damage to properties in close proximity has occurred, which would put corporate facilities in consequent danger or within an exclusion area imposed by the emergency services, an estimation of the possible exclusion period is essential. This will probably be undertaken on a 'best guess' basis by the property security or services manager, but a few words with the senior fire or police officer onsite may quickly clarify the picture.

Invocation of the business continuity plan

If, upon the basis of damage appraisal, it is decided by senior management or BC committee members to invoke the BC plan, the first stage in the recovery process will be to invoke occupation procedures (which are normally limited to a designated staff list) for the recovery site and inform the various departmental recovery teams. IT will normally be the first department to attend the recovery site in order to set up and configure PC systems in accordance with a predetermined facilities and time-based schedule which is dependent upon the needs of key user departments.

Business continuity control centre

23.1 LOCATION

The control centre should be located at a distance sufficiently removed from the damaged corporate site it is serving, so that it cannot be involved in the same disaster event. Conversely, it may be considered that to have the site too far away will make it difficult for staff to reach, both on the invocation when they may have to walk to it, as well as on a day-to-day basis. As the control centre acts as a liaison point between the recovery site from which the company is operating, the progressive establishment of additional services at that site and the reinstatement of the damaged site, ideally it should be situated adjacent to the recovery site and often takes the form of a conference room or suite within it.

23.2 ACTIVATION OF THE BC CONTROL CENTRE

Activation of the control centre can be instigated upon invocation of the business continuity plan by any member of the BC committee. Following this decision, the control centre will be in control of monitoring the recovery process. All external contacts will be made via the control centre in order that it may monitor progress, instigate all necessary action and correlate information for senior management.

23.3 CONTROL CENTRE TEAM

The control centre will be active 24 hours per day from invocation until full resumption of normal business operations at recovered or alternative long-term business sites. At this time, the decision will be made to progressively scale down control centre activities, although there is little doubt that a major incident will necessitate some staff involvement for many months, if not years.

23.3.1 Staffing

The control centre will need to be run by a small group of company staff who have both wide knowledge and experience of corporate operations, together with considerable involvement with business continuity practices. While all businesses will define their own priorities and staffing levels in line with their business practice, a number of points should be noted:

1 A senior manager without BC experience or training should not be included in control centre staff. Such a person may wish to control operations because of rank rather than ability.
2 Since the control centre is likely to function on a 24-hour basis for many days or weeks, there must therefore be sufficient staff available to allow suitable rest periods and holidays while maintaining satisfactory operational continuity.
3 As far as possible, staff should not be removed from critical business departments to work as part of the control centre team.

A typical control centre would comprise the following staff:

- a BC committee chairman
- two BC administrators
- an HR co-ordinator
- a property services co-ordinator
- an IT co-ordinator (technical)
- an IT co-ordinator (operational)
- a communications co-ordinator
- a property, security and insurance co-ordinator/advisor.

All control centre staff, probably working on a three-shift system, together with any deputies, must make necessary arrangements to be contactable at all times. The BC administrator is responsible for notifying and agreeing changes of control centre staff with the BC committee and for ensuring that those taking over the various roles are fully aware of their duties and responsibilities. The need for continuity is of paramount importance.

Exclusion from corporate sites — plans at departmental level

NOTE: Although included in the main text here to provide continuity, it has been found practical to retain this chapter separately in ring-binder form. (In order to facilitate this it is also available on the accompanying CD.) There are four reasons for this:

1 It enables easy update on a regular basis when there are changes of staff or other details.
2 It enables each department to readily review their needs and interdependencies with other departments.
3 It allows each member of staff to have their own copy of their departmental plan requirements and instructions (and they should be encouraged to take these home).
4 It allows an easy format for reference and update by the BC administrator, on a regular basis.

24.1 REQUIREMENTS, AVAILABLE FACILITIES AND MANAGEMENT INSTRUCTIONS FOR DEPARTMENTAL STAFF

Experience has shown that while it is possible to put equipment and service requirements into a standardized form for each department, managers prefer to write their own instructions, in consultation with their staff, so that these reflect their own best operating practices which are in a familiar terminology. This allows all levels of staff within a department to be completely familiar with their own plan details and confident that they know both what is expected of them and where they are supposed to be in a disaster situation. The practice has therefore developed where departmental requirements are defined on a grid table, as shown throughout this section, while procedural notes and instructions are recorded in a less rigid format. As demonstrated, these notes may be either very detailed and long or quite brief; the only criterion is whether they give sufficient information for staff to be fully conversant with their roles in an emergency situation. To this end it is advised that a member of the BC committee, conversant with a specific departmental operation, should review the notes to ensure that in the event that all key staff are incapacitated, others will be able to understand the notes and re-establish the department.

A variety of practical examples of this department-familiar text are shown in the following sections, but there is also a need for a practical and easily referenced index of departments, their priority levels and business continuity representatives. In the examples shown these have been combined into a reference grid which is defined by departmental cost code, but there is no reason why this should not be modified to best fit with individual business structures. It is, however, also important that interdependent departments agree on operating and emergency procedures and in what way this mutuality affects their risk levels; this may therefore also place a demand on the structure of the indexing system used.

It is apparent that, in such a collection of examples, there will be a great deal of repetition as each departmental area will, for example, document procedures for evacuation. This is unavoidable as experience has shown that staff are much more likely to refer to their own departmental section for guidance rather than a common procedures section. The repetitious areas have, as far as possible, been omitted from each departmental section, but included as a common example in the form of a preface. Once again it is emphasized that these examples are not intended to cover all possible departments in all working environments but rather to give a broad example of what has proved to be acceptable.

24.2 DEPARTMENTAL BUSINESS CONTINUITY INDEX

The following are intended as examples of departmental checklisting. It is likely that, with normal staff changes, this will require regular update as changes occur. The inclusion of a departmental cost code or similar referencing system will enable this list to be used as an index for the full departmental plan requirements which are detailed later.

24.3 PREFACE TO DEPARTMENTAL PLANS

24.3.1 Evacuation or exclusion from corporate sites

When staff are notified to leave their places of work in the event of regular fire drills or non-threatening incidents such as power failure or water leaks, it may not be necessary for initial evacuation to be at distant locations. In these cases 'short-term' assembly points can be convenient places where staff are collected and a roll-call taken before a decision is made whether to re-occupy the premises or whether there is a need to travel to more distant, longer-term assembly points. The following are examples* of initial assembly points:

Location	Assembly points
*Staff located at site A:	Car park at the back of site B
*Staff located at site B:	Car park at the back of site A

Dept. cost code	BC rep (name) deputy rep	All departments	Priority *	Contact home	24-hour contact (mobile)
1	A	Chief executives' office	1		
	B	Directors	2		
2		Human resources & post room	1		
3		Property & facilities services	1		
4		Computer operations & communications	1		
5		Public relations & marketing support	3		
6		Finance & accounts	1		
7		Sales & marketing	3		
8#		Purchasing	3		
9#		Insurance	1		
10#		Operations and support services	2		
11#		Manufacturing	2		
12#		Research & development	3		
13#		Transport	1		
Business continuity committee			1		

Priority★ represents the level of business criticality that is allocated to each department and the restart time frame requirement – for example, 1 = high, (full recovery within 4 hours); 2 = medium, (progressive recovery within 48 hours); 3 = low, (progressive recovery within 7 days.)

Not included as departmental examples.

(Pubs, cafes, main railway stations or public street areas are not good assembly points and should be avoided.)

If staff are told to evacuate their workplace, in the event of a genuine incident, the assembly points should be outside any zone of danger or possible exclusion area which is likely to be imposed by the emergency services. Ideally these will be somewhere sheltered with waiting, toilet, communication and refreshment facilities, as well as 'quiet' areas which may be used should trauma counselling be necessary. Hotels are favoured for this purpose but hotel staff tend to be transitory and it is critical to establish an agreement and maintain the continuity of contact, regularly notifying the hotel of any changes to the BC requirements. It is often most convenient to renew this contact just prior to a full business continuity test, but failing this, the BC administrator must ensure satisfactory facilities are maintained. Before establishing such an agreement with a specific hotel, it is important to verify that they do not have a similar contract with another business premises close to one's own as both businesses may then need the facility at the same time in the event of a common disaster event.

It is also common for hotels to have valuable commitments in their yearly calendar and the holding of a large convention at the time of a disaster invocation, whether as a test or actual incident, may well be a practical exclusion from agreed facilities. It is therefore strongly advised that a back-up hotel facility be considered which is not located near the first. Experience has shown that the use of a hotel group, rather than an individual hotel, is effectively able to circumvent such an eventuality.

The following should be added to the pages of each departmental plan so that it is not necessary for staff to refer to common references:

If site A or B is cordoned off, all staff will go to:

> The XXXX Hotel
> Full address,
> Full telephone number.

If site A or B and The XXXX Hotel is cordoned off, all staff will go to:

> The YYYY Hotel
> Full address
> Full telephone number

24.4 BUSINESS HOT START SITES

Upon evacuation from their place of work, staff should **not** go directly to the business 'hot start' site. At some early stage following an evacuation, there will be a need for BC management to agree whether it is necessary for invocation of the hot start site to be initiated, or whether a short waiting period is likely to enable re-occupation of the normal working premises.

While this decision process is in progress all staff should remain at the assembly point. If it is agreed that there is to be invocation of the BC hot start site, it is likely that only essential staff will initially be required, to reconfigure PC systems, set up relocated networks and, together with BC management and related staff, re-establish business functionality. Previous BC testing should give an accurate timescale for the recovery of essential business function availability and when other staff may therefore begin making their way to the BC site to resume business operations. Economic considerations would normally dictate that available work stations at hot start sites are not intended to replace all staff accommodation, but rather provide a core of essential operations which will preserve business functionality and maintain client confidence until such time as either the original site is reinstated or alternative long-term accommodation is provided.

Key departmental personnel should check their departmental procedures so they know who is required to attend the business hot start site and whether they are required at the site from day one.

The business continuity 'hot-start' site is located at:

Full address
Full telephone number

24.5 BUSINESS CONTINUITY HOT-SITE SEATING PLAN

(Full address)
Main telephone number

It is of considerable importance that, following an emergency invocation of the business recovery site, all staff should:

- know how to get to the BC site by various means
- know their desk allocation
- have PC access and specific system configuration where necessary
- have other facilities which will allow them to return to full functionality within the defined time frame.

Staff will not necessarily all work in the same office area, nor indeed in the same building, so it is therefore important that local telephone directories and site plans are available to all.

Example 1: Site A

Address

Telephone number (or direct extension)

Location on a site plan

Desk number	Name	Extension number
A1		XXXX
A2		XXXX

Example 2: Site B

Address

Telephone number (or direct extension)

Location on a site plan

Desk number	Name	Extension number
B1		YYYY
B2		YYYY

Example 3: Site C

Address

Telephone number (or direct extension)

Location on a site plan

Desk number	Name	Extension number
C1		ZZZZ
C2		ZZZZ
C98	Messengers/post room	ZZZZ
Conference room A	BC management/ control centre	Direct lines
		Extensions

24.6 EXAMPLES OF DEPARTMENTAL PLANS

24.6.1 Key personnel: chief executive officer (CEO) and directors

Priority 1: Cost code 1

Name	Home no.	Work no.	Mobile no.
CEO			
CEO staff			
Deputy CEO			
DCEO staff			

Business address and floor

Personnel	Day 1	Days 2 to 5	Between Day 6 and Day 20
CEO	✓	✓	✓
CEO staff	1 of 3	2 of 3	3 of 3
Deputy CEO	✓	✓	Split with CEO
Deputy CEO staff	1 of 5	All	All

Allocated desks and telephones in the BC management conference room. (No IT capability has been requested.)

24.6.2 Key personnel: human resources

Priority 1: Cost code 2

Name	Home no.	Work no.	Mobile no.
A			
B			
C			

List additional staff who may be asked to deputize in case of an emergency:

Business address and floor

Personnel (Name)	Day 1	Days 2 to 5	Between Day 6 and Day 20
A	✓	Any two of key staff (A, B, C) plus 50% of other staff	Any two of key staff (A, B, C) plus all normal staff
B	✓	Ditto	Ditto
C	✓	Ditto	Ditto

Available facilities	Day 1	Days 2 to 5	Between Day 6 and Day 20
Desks + PCs	2	3	5
Staff records	1	1	4
Staff pay records	1	2	4
Staff welfare records	1	2	4
Staff location and availability records	1	2	4
Other			
Special or dedicated PCs	1	2	2
Standard office software	1	3	5
Dedicated software (specify)	1	1	2
Internet link	1	1	1
Other software			
Telephones	2	3	3
Fax machine	1	1	1
Telex machine			

In the event of a serious incident, **A** and **B** will relocate to the hot start site.

From Day 2, **C** will be located at the hot start site in order to supervise the payroll service. **A** and **B** will also act as liaison between the rest of the HR staff and with the BC administrator.

Post room staff will fall under the management of HR during BC incidents and other HR staff will help to co-ordinate the distribution and delivery of mail to all BC sites via motorcycle/van services – using the existing courier company as far as possible.

Departmental instructions

Evacuation sites	**Assembly sites**
Staff located at site A:	Car park at the back of site B
Staff located at site B:	Car park at the back of site A

If site A or B is cordoned off, all staff will go to:

The XXXX Hotel
Full address
Full telephone number

If the area involved is so large that all of the sites A and B and The XXXX Hotel is cordoned off, all staff will go to:

The YYYY Hotel
Full address
Full telephone number
Directions to get there

Outside normal working hours

If a disaster occurs out of working hours, staff will be notified at home by the BC management team and advised to call the emergency 'freephone' number (a service provided by BT) at regular periods in order to obtain updated information. This will include details of: those required to return to work and where and when they should report; a brief update of the recovery progress and any other useful information.

The BC administrator will be responsible for ensuring that the emergency freephone messaging system is regularly updated.

During normal working hours

1 In the event of an emergency occurring during normal business hours staff will assemble at the initial evacuation site (address) and a roll-call will be taken by fire wardens in order to ensure all staff are safe.
2 At the point when a full-scale emergency is declared and the hot start site procedure is invoked, HR staff, other than those needed for BC purposes, will go to (address) Hotel together with all other non-essential Day 1 staff. Members of staff should not leave the initial assembly point until authorized in order to ensure that an accurate record of their whereabouts is maintained.
3 Once staff arrive at the hotel they will be advised whether or not they are needed or whether they can go home. If emergency funds are required for such items as warm clothing, travelling expenses, or the services of locksmiths to replace lost house or car keys, these will be obtained by HR management using an approved bank facility. Those advised to go home should be reminded of the emergency freephone number so they can call for updated information.
4 Staff not fit to travel home alone will need to be escorted by either a work colleague or first aid volunteer (see attached list). There will also be a facility for staff to remain at the hotel overnight or until collected by their families.

5 In the event that numbers of staff are severely traumatized, it may be necessary for HR staff to provide 24-hour coverage until matters have been resolved. A suitable rota will be established at the time depending upon staff availability. Where necessary, hotel accommodation will be provided for HR staff.

6 All liaison concerning missing or injured staff and their families will be instigated by the emergency services. HR will liaise with the company chief fire warden, who will be the contact with emergency services concerning the number and location of the injured.

The hospitals serving the company area and which are set up to take casualties are as follows:

Hospital A

Full address and telephone number

(First 6–20 casualties)

Then

Hospital B

Full address and telephone number

(Up to 80 casualties)

First aid wardens (Premises A)

First aid volunteers (Names)	Deputy	Responsible for
One	a	Basement
Two	b	Ground floor
Three	c	1st floor
Four	d	2nd floor
	(etc.)	

Fire wardens and deputies (premises A)

Chief fire warden

Fire warden	Deputy	Responsible for
		Basement
		Special area 1
		1st floor
	(etc.)	

(Special arrangements may be necessary for the senior management floor where there may be insufficient staff to fill these duties.)

Human resources (HR) procedures

1 Computerized files

All main HR files including the payroll system, are maintained on the IT network and should be available within four hours of invocation at the hot start site. If data is updated on a previous 24-hour basis rather than in live time, a contingency is therefore necessary for the possible loss of data during the 24-hour period immediately prior to the disaster event.

2 Essential records

Individual personnel files will usually be held in fire-resistant cabinets within the department and these will therefore not be immediately available in the event of an emergency.

Key policy documents relating to staff, such as those for pension or insurance schemes should be held in an offsite vault and copies made available as working documents where they are required.

3 Offsite storage

The HR department will require access to a secure storage facility at the BC hot start site. This can be used to store the staff handbook, procedure manuals and all main forms and letterheads which are not immediately available from printers or other company sites.

4 Payroll records

These should be backed up daily and will therefore be accessible once the main IT systems are operational at the hot start site. In the event of an emergency occurring at the time the payroll is due, a procedure should be established by the HR manager for the data to be sent or taken manually for processing to the company bank or other salary paying agency.

5 Employee contact details

These are normally held on the main computer system. Complete contact listings will need to be held by the HR manager and personal palm-top computers are useful for this purpose. These can be downloaded to a stand-alone PC at the hot start site if required. Departmental BC representatives will also need to hold listings of their departmental staff and a similar method can be used. In the event of a business continuity invocation out of hours, the duty BC management member of staff will inform the HR manager, who will use the listed contact details to contact all members of the BC team, departmental management and representatives.

6 Contingency staff operations

The HR team will be responsible for recording the whereabouts and the immediate welfare of all staff whether at the hotel, hot start site, hospital or at home.

It is envisaged that many of the normal day-to-day HR functions will not be required immediately following a disaster situation but wider operational and support functions will be required. These will include management of extended or 24-hour duty rotas, ensuring that satisfactory staff rest periods and breaks are maintained, assisting with difficult travelling arrangements, and continuing with staff support and counselling where necessary.

HR immediate contact details (examples only)

Health and safety executive	Telephone:
Full address and contact names	Fax:

Trauma counselling consultants	
Full address and contact names	Telephone:
	Fax:

Health insurance provider	
Full address and contact names	Telephone:
	Fax:

Health, welfare or other providers	Telephone:
	Fax:

Counselling

In the event of a crisis affecting staff at work, HR staff should institute the following procedure:

1 Draw up a list of staff involved in the crisis or affected by it. Talk with them to see if any assistance is required, and, if appropriate, contact a professional counselling service and arrange for meetings. It is also possible that immediate family members of injured or severely traumatized staff may need counselling help.

2 After a week has elapsed, those staff who have not returned to work should be contacted individually to see how they are coping, whether they need further assistance, or are unhappy with the assistance they have received to date. Liaison with the counselling providers must be maintained to determine levels of progress and whether alternatives are necessary.

3 It is essential that line managers form a link in the healing process and they should be in regular contact with their staff where this is welcomed. Line managers should also encourage the use of counselling services.

24.6.3 Key personnel: post room (as part of HR)

Priority 1: Cost code 2

Name	Home no.	Work no.
A		
B		
C		

Business address and floor

Personnel (Name)	Day 1	Days 2 to 5	Between Day 6 and Day 20
Manager	1	1 (shared)	Normal working
D/Manager	1	1 (shared)	Normal working
Other staff	100%	100%	Normal working

Services	Day 1	Days 2 to 5	Between Day 6 and Day 20
Desks	1	1	1
Large tables	4	4	6
Pigeon holes	50	50	100
Post bags	50	50	100
Packing materials	Collect from supplier	Daily delivery	Daily delivery
Franking machine	1	1	1
PCs	1	1	1
MS Office software	1	1	1
Marketing software	1	1	1
Telephones	1+1 mobile	1+1 mobile	1+1 mobile
Fax machine	1	1	1
Colour copies	1	1	1

Departmental instructions

Should it be necessary to evacuate either of the corporate sites at (addresses), arrangements have been made for all mail to be redirected to (address). Post room staff will be accommodated at this site with the equipment scheduled on the previous page.

At the time of the incident the post room manager or his deputy will co-ordinate the redirection, distribution and delivery of mail to all BC sites via the post office or couriers.

Until temporary sorting and other equipment is made available onsite, incoming post will be sorted on the large tables provided in preparation for distribution to the temporary operational and business continuity sites. Delivery to these sites will be undertaken by the normal contracted courier service (contact name, address, telephone number).

These couriers will also collect outgoing post and deliver it to the normal sorting office each evening in order to ensure overnight delivery. Until a franking machine is available the post room manager will arrange for suitable quantities of stamps to be purchased on a daily basis. The post room manager will obtain cash for stamps and other essential purchases from the HR manager.

24.6.4 Key personnel: property and facilities management

Priority 1: Cost code 3

Name	Home no.	Work no.	Mobile no.
A			
B			
C			

Business address and floor

Personnel	Day 1	Days 2 to 5	Between Day 6 and Day 20
A (Manager)	✓	✓	✓ Working rota with deputy
B (Deputy manager)	✓	✓	✓ Working rota with manager
Administrator	✓	✓	✓ Normal working
Staff (10)	✓ (all)	✓ (on 24-hour shift rota)	✓ (Rota as agreed with manager)

Services	Day 1	Days 2 to 5	Between Day 6 and Day 20
Desks/chairs	2	2	3
Mobile telephones	3	3	3
2-way radios	10	10	10
Protective clothing	12	12	12
Agreed emergency	6	6	6
Tool kits/lighting			
Key cutting facilities	1	1	1
PCs	1	1	1
MS Office software	1	1	1
Specialist software for premises plans	1	1	1
Telephones	3	3	3
Fax machine	1 (shared)	1 (shared)	1 (shared)
Large format printer	1	1	1

As a great deal of departmental data does not lend itself to IT storage, essential original documentation is stored in a secure offsite data facility (address) and working copies are stored at corporate sites _____, which are in the custody of _____.

Initially, facilities management staff will be housed at the hot start facility. As soon as possible following the incident, all other departmental staff will be based in temporary accommodation as close to the damaged site as possible.

Departmental instructions

1 Disaster invocation during normal work hours

a) The XXX Hotel is the closest convenient assembly point to the evacuated corporate premises. All departmental staff will remain at this point until given further instructions. Duties, dependent upon the type and scope of the incident, may include:

- security of the site once it has been released by the emergency services and prior to its re-occupation by staff or a guarding force
- searching the premises in the case of a suspect object being reported
- assessment of the damaged site.

b) The departmental administrator will be accommodated at the hot start site, and liaise with departmental staff, management and contractors as well as managing normal correspondence.

2 Disaster invocation out of normal work hours

a) The departmental BC administrator will maintain an up-to-date call-out list of all departmental personnel and liaise closely with the HR manager for this purpose.

b) Staff must be aware of the location and quickest method of reaching each corporate site out of normal business hours.

c) The departmental BC administrator will have access to information via the PC network concerning premises, plans, all contracts and leases. Original contracts and leases are held in secure storage and are not normally available but true copies are immediately available from the facilities manager if required.

3 Agreements have been established with a number of building companies to ensure that a general facility is always available for emergency work such as hoarding construction, plumbing and electrical repair. Please refer to the emergency list for company details and the scope of the business continuity facilities they are able to supply.

4 Those members of the facilities staff who are likely to be employed at the damaged site must ensure that they are in possession of their safety and protective equipment and that their mobile telephones and torches are regularly charged and maintained.

External maintenance contractors
Full address

Telephone numbers

Scope of services provided

During normal working hours telephone numbers

(Contact names)

Outside normal working hours telephone numbers

(Contact names)

When calling external contractors, ensure that the following details are documented in the log-book provided, as these will be required for costing and insurance claims.

1 Phone number of contractor

2 Company name

3 Company address

4 Contract number (only available to authorized members of staff)

5 Nature of problem

6 Person to whom spoken

7 Date and time of call

Note: The contractor will provide alternative day and night numbers in order that contact can be guaranteed.

24.6.5 Key personnel: computer operations (IT) and communications

Priority 1: Cost code 4

	Name	**Home no.**	**Work no.**
Head of:			
IT			
Systems			
Computer operations			
Applications			
Communications			
Technical services			
Company branches			
Other key staff			

IT systems, operations, applications, technical services and communications
Business address and floor

Personnel	Day 1*	Days 2 to 5*	Between Day 6 and Day 20
Systems	All	All	Normal working
Operations	All	All	Normal working
Applications	All	4	Normal working
Technical services	All	4	Normal working

Services	Day 1	Days 2 to 5	Between Day 6 and Day 20
Desks	4	11	Same
Data transmission routes	2	4	All
PCs	4	11	11
Printers	2	4	4
Alternative transmission routes	4	4	4
Specialist PCs	1	2	2
Office software	4	11	11
Specialist software	1	2	2
Telephones	12	12	12
Fax machine	1	1	1
Photocopier	1	1	1
Telex terminal	1	1	1
Telex printer	1	1	1
Telex lines	2	2	2
Modem phone lines	10	11	11

* It may be necessary to introduce shift work in order to give 24-hour coverage, draft in staff from other corporate computer sites or employ suitable contractors.

Departmental instructions

In the event of a disaster, the BC administrator will notify the head of IT, and the managers of systems, operations, technical support and development. The administrator will then initiate calls to the hot site recovery operators and put them on notice that invocation is to take place.

Computer operators

The operations supervisors will be contacted by the systems and operations manager and be informed of the nature of the disaster. All computer operators involved in the recovery process will relocate to the hot start site and begin initial PC set-up procedures.

The full address of the recovery site is:

(Full address of recovery site)

In the early stages of recovery while PCs are being set up it is highly likely that 24-hour working will be necessary. IT supervisors will therefore establish suitable operator shift rotas. The operations supervisors will also be responsible for collecting the offsite back-up tapes from secure storage and take them to the hot start site. Once PCs are available at the hot start site, the initial build and configuration procedures will take place in order to re-create the designated corporate operating and database systems.

Systems and communications specialists

The systems and operations managers will inform systems and communications specialists of the nature of the disaster and they will assist with setting up back-up systems at the hot start site. Once this has been completed they will start sourcing replacement equipment and software for the less critical systems.

PC support

Once the initial system set-up is complete, support staff will cover all sites, installing and configuring replacement equipment as required. Shift rotas and additional travelling expenses will be made available and managed by HR.

Applications

One member of the development team will go to the hot start site to assist with any problems arising with bespoke corporate systems.

Requirements

Once systems have been set up, IT systems and operations staff will require desks and PCs to maintain the various systems and run a help desk support for staff.

24.6.6 Communications (as part of IT)

Priority 1: Cost code 4

Name	Home no.	Work no.
A		
B		

Business address and floor

Personnel	Day 1	Days 2 to 5	Between Day 6 and Day 20
A	1	1	Normal duty
B	1	1 + contract staff where necessary	Normal duty + contract staff

Services	Day 1	Days 2 to 5	Between Day 6 and Day 20
Desks	1 + 1	1 + 1	2 + 1
Dedicated transmission lines	2	2	2 + 1
Dedicated printer*	1	1	1
Dedicated software	1	1	1
PCs	1	1	1 + 1
Office software	1	1	1
Corporate network link	1	1	1
PC printer	1	1	1
Telephones	2	2	6
Fax machine	2	2	2
Photocopier	1	1	1
Telex lines	4	4	4
Modem phone lines	2	2	2
Telex terminals/printers */**	2	2	2

* Additional printers may be required if all internal and external telecommunication requirements are to be routed via the communications department.

** Additional telex terminals and printers may be required if dedicated transmission cables are unavailable.

Departmental instructions

1 Disaster invocation during normal work hours

a) Upon notification by the BC administrator or IT operations manager, members of the communications department will travel to the hot start site as soon as they are able, following release from the assembly point.

b) In the event of 24-hour cover being required to manage re-routing and initial manual handling of data transmission, HR will provide suitable contract staff.

2 Disaster invocation out of normal work hours

a) The BC administrator will contact communications staff who will then travel to the hot start site as directed.

b) In the event of 24-hour cover being required, HR will provide cover as in 1b above.

Equipment

In a disaster situation, all necessary equipment, which must be listed in the contract with the hot start provider, will be made available within four hours of invocation.

Procedures

All departmental procedures should be detailed and alternative procedure flow charts included which show interdependencies with the IT department and their effects should further facilities become unavailable. Copies of critical interactive flow charts will be made available to the BC co-ordinator.

24.6.7 Key personnel: public relations and marketing support

Priority 3: Cost code 5

Name	Home no.	Work no.
A		
B		

Business address and floor

Personnel	Day 1	Days 2 to 5	Between Day 6 and Day 20
A	1	1	Normal duty
B (deputy)	1	1	Normal duty

Services	Day 1	Days 2 to 5	Between Day 6 and Day 20
Desks	1	1	1
TOBAS	1	1	1
PCs	1	1	1
MS Office software	1	1	1
Marketing software	1	1	1
Telephones	1	1	1
Fax machine	1	1	1
Bespoke software	1	1	1

On Day 1, one member of staff will be accommodated at a suitable facility where clients, members of the public and the press can be met. The PR department has a number of key roles to fulfil in the event of a major disaster taking place and should be able to mitigate the potential long-term loss of public confidence and help retain corporate market share.

Crisis public relations

There are five main areas of media which would need to be considered in the event of a crisis:

1 the international press
2 the western general newspapers
3 the US press
4 those areas where there are major corporate clients and operations
5 the specialist (trade) press.

There is also a need to reassure:

1 the institutional client base*
2 shareholders*
3 potential new clients
4 staff.

*Specific telephone calls or faxes from marketing/public relations to clients and major shareholders.

The following actions would need to be taken:

1 Produce 'holding statements' for clients covering revised production/supply schedules.
2 Assemble a crisis team and keep clients updated.
3 Produce situation assessments of likely timescales for staged recovery.
4 Decide a basic text for an initial press release.
5 Hold regular briefing meetings with the CEO's office.
6 Arrange press conferences at regular intervals and advise senior management on a likely corporate representative who would face the press.

In the event of a disaster no press statement should be released without express permission of the group CEO or deputy.

Departmental instructions

The head of the public relations team will, in consultation with the CEO, collect all necessary departmental update information and write all press releases.

24.6.8 Key personnel: finance and accounts

Priority 1: Cost code 6

Name	Home no.	Work no.
A		
B		
C		

* Depending upon the size of the business concerned, it may be necessary to further subdivide this department and expand the documented requirements (below). However, the primary concern is that all financial departments are comprehensively protected and are able to maintain full functionality irrespective of the scale of a disaster. It is not unknown for corporate clients to delay payment in the hope that relevant records may have been destroyed in a major incident.

Business address and floor

Personnel	Day 1	Days 2 to 5	Between Day 6 and Day 20
Senior finance and accounting staff	At least two from each department	50% or shift	Normal working
Junior accounts staff	Team leaders	Shift	Shift

Services	Day 1	Days 2 to 5	Between Day 6 and Day 20
Desks	To increase with staff complement	Junior staff to be accommodated	Department should be fully functional
PCs	As desks	As desks	As desks
Office software			
Accounts software			
Invoice software			
Printers			
Invoice printing system			
PC links/stock controls			
Specialist equipment			
Telephones			
Fax machine			
Other equipment			

Departmental instructions

The following procedures are to be invoked if there is a disaster that prevents access to the normal place of work.

The initial assembly point, following evacuation is:

(a) _____

Alternative

(b) _____

Remote site

If the normal place of work is likely to be unavailable for more than a few hours, a contract is in place to provide staff with an alternative office facility. This facility provides PCs, telephones, relevant data links and other equipment in accordance with the schedule above. From Day 2, most PCs will have relevant departmental software but less critical systems, such as that for printing invoices, are not expected to be available until Day 3. **Not all staff will be accommodated at this site from Day 1 and some will remain at home and await further instructions**. Information will be available to everyone on the freephone number.

Disaster invocation out of normal work hours

If the disaster occurs at night or at the weekend, management would be informed by the disaster recovery administrator and will themselves disseminate information further to their own departmental members and decide who will be required to attend.

Duty rotas and shift working requirements will be reviewed during Day 1 by departmental management and arrangements will be made to ensure that adequate coverage is provided as necessary.

Availability of file back-up

- All accounts files are backed up on a daily basis and would be made available at the hot start site within four hours. However, should a disaster strike overnight, the PC back-up tape would not be retrieved and the data would be one day out of date. For this reason a member of the departmental staff has been appointed to take a copy of each day's work home to ensure that the full transaction database may be restored without undue problems.
- Clients' historical files are stored on optical disk and copies are held offsite. These files are updated regularly, at three-month intervals.
- The client credit and order databases are backed up and will be available to staff within two days. Individual client files and contact information must also be stored either in fireproof cabinets or on the optical archiving facility within the department. CDs must be stored offsite each evening.

Business cards and other 'personal' filing is the responsibility of the individuals concerned.

All departmental staff

Staff are responsible for their own business documents, files and diaries and must ensure that nothing of business value is left on desktops overnight. Where required, documents should be stored in fireproof filing cabinets or duplicated on CD and stored offsite.

Staff are also responsible for advising the departmental secretary of any changes of home address, phone number or anything which may inhibit the ability for rapid staff contact and therefore the effectiveness of the proposed business continuity planning.

Disaster recovery facts (part of finance and accounts)

Day of disaster (Day 0) during normal working hours

All staff to evacuate and meet at assembly points, and remain there until further instructions.

Assembly point	
(a) address	*A bomb threat or assembly at site (a) is impractical for the following reasons:
OR (b) address*	
	Re-occupation of the worksite is unlikely to be within two+ hours Severe weather conditions at site (a) Innovation of disaster recover procedures because of fire/flood etc.

Fire wardens have responsibility for:

• recording staff presence at the assembly points
• reporting missing persons to emergency services and to HR department
• providing initial first aid assistance, as necessary.

(Day 1)

Hot start sites

(Full address)

(List of staff)

The above individuals will be allocated desks.

ALL OTHER STAFF must remain at home until called.

(Day 2)

(Full address of location or alternatives)

(It is likely that lists of staff can only be drawn up once senior staff have assessed the limits of the disaster situation and how it has affected functionality. However, a provisional list may be included if it would help in 'layering' the response and preparedness of staff.)

24.6.9 Key personnel: sales and marketing

Priority 1: Cost code 7

Name	Home no.	Work no.
A		
B		
C		

Large sales and marketing departments can require severe 'pruning' during times of disaster as manufacturing processes may have been disrupted thus affecting the ability to supply clients. This is likely to remain in force until production or the broader business continuity picture has stabilized.

Business address and floor

Services	Day 1	Days 2 to 5	Between Day 6 and Day 20
Desks	11	11	12
PCs with Windows™	11	11	12
Incoming printer	1	1	1
Outgoing printer	1	1	1
Default printer	1	1	1
PC network printer	1	1	1
Direct dial phones	11	11	12
Client database	1	1	1
Marketing database	1	1	1
Manufacturing database	1	1	1
Stock position database			
Other specialist databases			
Fax machine	3	3	3

Departmental instructions

1 Disaster invocation during normal work hours

All staff will assemble in the designated area _____. The fire wardens will perform a roll-call ensuring the attendance of every member of staff. All staff are to remain at the assembly point until the situation has been clarified. Should we be unable to return to work, the BC administrator and the key personnel will direct staff to the relevant locations. The table below shows the personnel required to remain at work, their responsibilities and location. Should any member of staff be absent or incapacitated, then the person(s) shown in the last column of the table will be required to provide cover.

2 Disaster invocation out of normal work hours

The BC administrator will contact key personnel and advise them of the situation. Key personnel will then telephone each member of the group for whom they are responsible, advising them of the location for the first working day and whether they are required or not. The table below shows the required staffing levels and their responsibilities for the first day of business recovery. Staff not required for work on the first day should contact the freephone information line on a daily basis. Staff must avoid using the normal switchboard or direct numbers as this may overwhelm the limited telephone service available.

3 Procedures for the days following a disaster

On the days following the initial recovery, spaces for (11) people have been allocated to this department. In order to take full advantage of the equipment and space available, a shift system has been devised which is broadly based on the closing times of the UK, eastern and western international markets. The attached tables broadly describe the responsibilities of each member of staff, the times they will be required to work and their location.

Day 1 names	Day 1 duties
Manager	External communications, general support and guidance
Deputy manager	As above
A	
B	
C	
D	
E	
All other staff	Available for cover
Day 2 names	**Day 2 duties**
As Day 1	As Day 1

Sales and marketing telephone list

Personnel	Home tel no.	Mobile no.
Disaster information	Freephone number	

Appendix 1

Actions to be taken on receipt of a bomb threat (by telephone)

(Examples only)

If possible, immediately inform someone else but do not put down the handset or cut off the caller. A brief note to a colleague is the most commonly advised method.

Switchboard operators should record the entire conversation if they have suitable equipment and the following details can be used as an aid to suitable questions. (It is important to remain as conversational as possible.) Switchboard operators who do not have recording facilities will need to complete the following form in writing as best they can:

- the message (exact words)
- where is it?
- what time will it go off?
- what does it look like?
- what type of explosive is it?
- why are you doing this?
- who are you?
- anything else you can get – play it by ear
- date and time of call.

To be completed immediately upon completion of call:

- Details of caller (tick)

  (1) man   (3) child   (5) unknown

  (2) woman   (4) old/young

- Speech

    (1) intoxicated   (4) irrational

    (2) speech impediment   (5) rambling

    (3) serious   (6) laughing

- Accent

- was the message read or spontaneous?

- Distractions

    (1) noise on the line   (4) private phone

    (2) operator   (5) mobile phone

    (3) anyone in background (6) interruptions

- Pay phone

- Other noises

    (1) traffic   (4) machinery   (7) children

    (2) talking   (5) aircraft   (8) other

    (3) typing   (6) music

- Person receiving the call _____

- Telephone number on which the call was received _____

- Indication of telephone number from which the call was made _____

When the call has finished, the information should be passed by the switchboard operator, via the emergency conference call telephone system, to all senior managers available, who will decide what action should be taken. In addition, the switchboard will immediately inform those responsible for evacuation procedures. All evacuation messages to staff and visitors should be broadcast via the public address system operated by the switchboard. The more information obtained from a caller, the easier it will be to decide whether the warning was genuine or not, and what appropriate action to take.

A model company bomb incident plan

(Example only)

CONFIDENTIAL

TO: All staff members and for inclusion in staff handbook

FROM: The general manager

SUBJECT: Information and procedures concerning bomb threats and explosions

A bomb threat against company premises may be received by telephone or letter. Telephone threats may be received at the switchboard, in administrative offices or even be directed to the home telephone numbers of staff. Any member of staff receiving a telephone bomb threat should make every effort to follow the procedure outlined below:

THE BOMB THREAT

Most bomb threat calls are very brief. The caller normally states the message in a few words and rings off without actually entering into conversation. However, where possible every effort should be made to obtain detailed information from the caller, such as:

- exact location of the bomb
- time of detonation
- description of the explosive device
- type of explosive
- the reason for the threat or call.

The person receiving the call should also note such details about the call as:

- exact date and time of the call
- exact words used
- sex of the caller
- estimated age of the caller
- any peculiar or identifiable accent
- possible nationality of the caller
- identifiable background noises such as music, vehicles, trains and so on.

BOMB THREAT CHECKLIST

A bomb threat checklist has been prepared to assist members of staff to record information about such calls. A copy of this list is attached and should be kept handy at all times. Further copies can be obtained from the human resources department. Those members of staff who are able to record telephone conversations by means of their hand-held memo recorders are asked to do so in the eventuality of such a call as even a poor quality recording may well give more information than that which you are able to transcribe during a brief call.

When a bomb threat call is received, alert a colleague and, while keeping the caller in conversation, complete a 'bomb threat checklist' as fully as possible or record the message. Then report the call IMMEDIATELY to one of the following locations:

1 During office hours   Main switchboard   (telephone)

                                     Guard

                                     Other

                                     Office

2 Outside office hours   BC Administrator   (telephone/mobile/pager)

                                     Guard

                                     Other

                                     Individual

3 Emergency if (1) or (2) cannot be contacted (cascade list)

                                     Cascade 1, 2, 3 etc.   (telephone/office/mobile/home)

                                     Others

                                     Individual

4 If none of the above can be contacted, or a threat call is received at home, dial 999 and inform police.

Threats received by letter should be preserved for the police and fingerprint examination. Letters and envelopes should be retained in a large envelope or plastic bag, and should not be handled once the contents are known. Store the letter in a safe place for collection by the police. They will require a list of everyone who has handled such a letter so make a list before you forget.

In the event of a bomb threat being received, a preliminary decision will be made, in liaison with the police and management, with respect to the necessity for searching or evacuating the building. The procedures to be followed for each of two possible courses of action are summarized below.

NB It is essential that the police are informed immediately of any bomb threat. This will normally be carried out by the switchboard operator calling 999.

1 Searching the building without evacuation

If the preliminary decision is to search the building without evacuating staff, the following announcement will be made via the public address system:

> On the instructions of general management, all members of staff are asked to immediately carry out the bomb threat instruction by checking their offices and other parts of the building. Report any suspicious objects to the switchboard and keep other people away.

Upon receiving such an announcement, every fire warden and BC representative should arrange for staff to conduct a prompt visual search of the room/s for which he/she is responsible (see*1 and *2 below) and telephone the switchboard with any information concerning items or containers which are unusual, not in a logical place or cannot be accounted for. If all is found to be in order (remember that lives are at risk) inform the switchboard that all is secure. If an unaccounted or suspicious item is found do not try to move or handle it in any way. A call to the switchboard will cause the operator to instigate evacuation procedures by informing management of the situation and notifying emergency services.

> Location *1. Requires full listing of premises by the property facilities management.
> Personnel assigned *2. Appropriate staff to be assigned by HR department.

It is critical that EVERY area is included and assigned.

Non-company vehicles parked in unusual places SHOULD NOT BE APPROACHED. Their location and index numbers should be reported to switchboard staff.

2 Evacuation of the building

If the primary decision is to evacuate the building, the following announcement will be made via the public address system:

> On the instructions of general management you are informed that a bomb threat has been received which makes it necessary for everyone to leave the building immediately. Please leave your place of work, taking with you all your personal possessions ONLY if they are readily available, and proceed in the same manner as for a fire drill. Move to the prescribed place of safety and remain there until further instructions are given. A roll-call will be taken and anyone not at the prescribed assembly point will be searched for. This is not a drill.

On receiving such an announcement, fire wardens need to ensure that personnel know the proper exits to use when leaving the building. Fire wardens will check that all personnel have left the area for which they are responsible and conduct a brief search of the area for unusual objects. Staff members with special assignments such as shutting drawers or removing computer disks will complete this on their way out. If the task cannot be completed without delay no attempt should be made and the premises should be left at once.

Upon satisfying themselves that evacuation and preliminary searching has been completed, searchers will notify BC administration accordingly.

3 Protection within the building

If there is the real threat of a car bomb or similar device in the street, it may be thought safer, after consultation with police, to remain within the security of the building until the danger is over. The decision will be announced via the public address system, and the message will be as follows:

> On the instruction of general management, you are informed that a bomb threat has been received which indicates the device is outside the building, possibly in the street. It is necessary for everyone to leave their place of work and move to the central core of the building, which is the basement. Fire wardens and/or BC representatives will direct you to safe areas. Close all doors behind you and keep away from all windows and areas of glass. Please take all your personal possessions with you only if they are readily available. Remain at the prescribed place of safety until further instructions are given. A roll-call will be taken and anyone not at the prescribed assesmbly point will be searched for.

4 Detonation of a device, sudden impact of a vehicle or sudden eruption of a large fire

In the event of such an event without prior threat or during an evacuation, the emergency services will be immediately informed by any means possible, such as breaking a fire alarm call point, but this would be the primary responsibility of the switchboard staff irrespective of their location.

All personnel within the building at the time of such an event will evacuate the building by whatever means possible and go to their assembly point if they are able.

The HR manager or deputy will liaise with police and other emergency and medical services to carry out the following:

- identify those who have died
- identify those who are missing
- identify those who are injured or in shock
- take personnel related incoming calls
- make funds immediately available in order that emergency aid, such as hot meals, drinks, train and taxi fares, hotel accommodation and clothing, as appropriate can be given.

NB The next of kin of casualties will be notified by the police.

Appendix 3

Exclusion zone street plans

Street plans for exclusion zones (marked to show the size of possible exclusion sites)

Corporate site A

Corporate site B

EXCLUSION ZONES

In the event of a terrorist attack or other major incident, the likely exclusion zones which would be imposed by police cordoning are as follows:

1 An initial cordon of 100 metres radius. The cordon area would not be circular and would follow convenient roads and intersections. This may be all that is required in a fire situation but would be expanded to 400 metres in the case of a terrorist incident.
2 Unless an actual explosion dictated otherwise, an outer cordon of 600 metres radius would be formed in the same manner.

Police and emergency service vehicles normally park between the two cordon areas and, although civilian entry may be possible into the outer cordon area relatively quickly following an incident, the inner cordon area could be severely restricted for some considerable time, until it is considered safe to shrink it progressively. The level of safety may relate to secondary terrorist devices or dangerous buildings and falling glass. The cordoned areas can be very large and it is not always practical for police to control such perimeters.

Appendix 4

Evacuation sites

Corporate premises sites A and B. (This must be duplicated for all sites which come under this plan.)

If site A only is evacuated, staff meeting point:

Car park at the back of site B

If site B only is evacuated, staff meeting point:

Car park at the back of site A

If both sites are evacuated, all staff to go to:

The XXX Hotel
(Full address, telephone number and directions)
Main contact (manager)
Direct tel. no.
Or (deputy manager)
Direct tel. no.

If the XXX Hotel is cordoned off, all staff to go to:

The YYY Hotel
(Full address, telephone number and directions)
Main contact (manager)
Direct tel. no.
Or (deputy manager)
Direct tel. no.

All staff who are designated a place at the hot start site will go to:

Full address, telephone number and directions
Main contact name

Appendix 5

Local area searchers

Those who have volunteered to search their work areas for possible explosive or incendiary devices.

Corporate site A

(Full address)

Floor   Searchers   Deputy searchers

Search plans

Plans of premises divided into a grid system for bomb 'search and secure' purposes.

Corporate premises A

Corporate premises B

Appendix 7

Staff search groups

Staff able to initiate protective procedures in the case of a suspect postal bomb.

Names   Floor

(Any premises search will be carried out by BC reps, fire wardens, facilities management staff, and post room staff as appropriate.)

Business continuity committee

The mix and size of a BC committee may vary widely depending on the corporate requirement and size. The following is an example:

- a committee chairman
- two BC administrators
- an HR co-ordinator
- a property services co-ordinator
- an IT co-ordinator (technical)
- an IT co-ordinator (operational)
- a communications co-ordinator
- a property, security and insurance co-ordination/advisor.

Appendix 9

Business continuity representatives

Each department should have a minimum of two BC representatives and these should be listed, together with their work department and all available telephone numbers.

Name   Department   Location   Telephone

(Deputy)

Appendix 10

Senior management list

There is a potential need for the BC committee to be in contact with members of senior management on a 24-hour basis in order that policy decisions, meetings with bankers and insurers, and the sanctioning of significant expenditure can be undertaken. There is also a need for an appropriate 'corporate face' to be available at press conferences. It is therefore necessary that senior management provide their home and mobile telephone numbers for this purpose. There is an obvious potential security problem with making such a list, but it may be overcome by providing each member of the senior management group with an emergency mobile telephone, each of which has the same number. This would allow a single telephone number to be available for any emergency and negate the need to give personal details or even names.

Appendix 11

Key personnel lists

There is a need to combine all staff who appear on the various departmental 'key personnel' lists into a single document, which includes telephone numbers. It is imperative that there is good communications during and after any major emergency in order that staff are able to contact each other quickly.

Appendix 12

Keyholder lists

It is essential that, as a normal part of premises housekeeping, sets of keys are held offsite for use in emergency situations. This has already become an established practice with guarding companies that attend client premises in the event of an alarm activation outside of normal business hours. However, for use following a major fire or similar incident, keys to fireproof cabinets, vaults, desks, lockers and a great many other secure storage units may be required and these are not within the normal scope of a keyholding company. A facility should be made available for the secure offsite storage of a complete set of keys for all lockable items in each corporate site. While a bank-type safe deposit box may appear the obvious answer to the security storage aspect, consideration should be given to the fact that not all banks will give 24-hour, 365-day access to such facilities.

Appendix 13

Insurance details

(Include all if there is more than one.)

Insurance company name and address

Telephone number

Emergency telephone number

Contact names

Emergency telephone numbers for contact names

Policy name and type

Policy no.

Scope and limit of indemnity

The business continuity hot start site

Full address

Telephone number

Out of hours/emergency telephone number

Contact name(s)

How to get there (road, public transport or on foot)

Sketch plan

Bus numbers

Railway stations

Taxi availability

Walking distance

Appendix 15

Postscripts and general points for BC committee members

Insurance statistics concerning major incidents contain many recurrent problems that may be avoided by appropriate action being taken. The following are typical and staff involved with disaster recovery must be aware of them and act accordingly.

1 Know the landlord (or his agent where appropriate) as well as any neighbouring businesses. The scene of a disaster is neither the time nor place to make an initial contact or be on unfamiliar terms with these groups. The severe strain of any major crisis and loss of sleep makes it easy for most reasonable people to be difficult, but this is considerably diminished by a familiar face, a shared objective and recognized goals. A good relationship with the landlord and neighbouring businesses is worth the time spent but it should not be forgotten that the same pre-established relationship is equally important with police, fire and other emergency services.

2 Know the insurance brokers and establish a working relationship with them and their assessors. Ensure that business insurance contains a 'continuous business' clause, which underwrites costs for leasing temporary quarters and furnishing and maintaining a communications system.

3 Keep updated lists of computer, communications, leasing, printing and insurance companies and so on. When equipment, stationery and photocopiers are in ashes it is frequently very difficult to identify the current suppliers.

4 As far as possible, ensure essential documentation is afforded the protection of fireproof cabinets. Corporate policy and practice should ensure that desks are not being used as convenient alternatives.

5 Ensure that clients are not greeted with an 'unobtainable' telephone line. Facilities for immediate call diverting or forwarding are readily available from main telecommunications suppliers and this will help to maintain client confidence.

6 Ensure that all computer data and electronic document storage files are duplicated and either stored offsite or are automatically backed up to another server offsite. Time is well spent investigating what information is

deemed critical for effective business continuity, and how long it is stored locally (the retention period) before being backed-up offsite. Live time back-up is ideal but older systems may only back-up at more infrequent periods or even overnight out of business hours. This may therefore make the most recent corporate data vulnerable to complete loss, which would not be retrievable at the BC hot start site.

7 The BC committee members should have a good working relationship, and be both enthusiastic and knowledgeable about their roles. As soon as the nature of the crisis becomes clear (fire, flood, bombing, power cut, etc.) the committee must convene immediately and decide upon near-term objectives.

8 Action by the BC committee must follow logical steps in accordance with contingent action lists; but no emergency situation is likely to go exactly to plan and part of the plan must be to recognize the potential for necessary modification at short notice. Actions must aim at minimizing the effects of the emergency situation, ensuring the safety of all staff and maintaining business continuity. It is essential that quick and decisive action is taken to dispel doubts, maintain client confidence and avoid loss of business. Analysis of previous disasters strongly suggests that client confidence declines rapidly if (a) there is a failure to take immediate and strong management action, and (b) there is a failure of senior management to make frequent press statements, detailing the measures being taken.

9 In the case of fire, the fire brigade will make available to police, insurers or representatives of the losers or victims copies of their reports as part of an investigation into causation. However, corporate victims or others involved in such incidents may wish to employ the services of specialist fire investigators to establish the causation. The process of incident investigation will be benefited considerably by preserving the scene of damage until it has been fully documented, photographed and examined. Once a forensic examination has been completed, company representatives should conduct a room-by-room inventory of damage, covering furniture, equipment, personal effects and files. The evidence produced by a video recording and verbal commentary to support a massive insurance claim and to obviate any suggestion of 'negligent origin' of fire could be very cost effective.

10 Sites of disaster attract the ghoulish and the thief. It is important to secure the site with guards prior to the erection of suitable fencing. It will be necessary to have 24-hour guarding on most disaster sites and attempted entry by thieves can be expected.

11 It is essential to meet regularly with both landlord, neighbours and the local council in order to establish that clear-up is being carried out as quickly as possible and without further inconvenience to neighbours or the public.

Appendix 16

Essential telephone numbers (examples)

Address, telephone number and contact names for

Insurers

Press agents

Police stations, fire stations and hospitals

(Those with responsibility for the areas in which corporate premises are located)

Company doctors

Trauma counsellors

Ministers of the church

Salvage teams

Names, departments, telephone extensions and mobile numbers.

In the event of a major incident it may be necessary for these staff to enter corporate premises while a police or fire brigade cordon is still in operation. The emergency services will only allow entry to personnel wearing identification specific to this task. A list of those undertaking this work should be made available to the relevant authorities at the time by a designated member of the BC committee.

Appendix 18

Specialist companies

The following are examples of services provided by specialist companies, in disaster situations:

- decontamination, restoration and recovery project management
- drying services
- waste management
- emergency power
- high technology equipment preservation and transportation
- temporary business accommodation.

Part 3

Site Recovery and Salvage

Introduction

When damage to a corporate site is very severe, all too frequently the corporate 'mind' concentrates only on the primary objective of establishing business functionality at a new location. In consequence, the damaged site is frequently left with insufficient security, protection from the elements or planning for the urgent requirements of reclamation, whether this be data, documents, equipment, valuables, or the property itself. If further loss or damage is to be avoided and a successful association with insurers is to be established, it is critical that satisfactory site salvage management is put into place.

25.1 CORDONED OFF AREAS

In the event of a bomb detonation, major fire, traffic accident, gas leak or other incident, the area will be cordoned off by police to a distance of between 100 and 600 yards radius, dependent upon the nature, severity or likely effects. The area covered is relatively arbitrary, and is the responsibility of the senior police or fire officer present. No good purpose will be served by remonstrating with local police officers who are enforcing the boundary.

25.2 CITY SURVEYOR

Following the completion of work by the emergency services, the area may be in the control of the local authority and its surveyors who will conduct preliminary examinations for safety. When areas are declared safe, police will conduct required forensic examinations if a criminal act is suspected.

25.3 KEY PERSONNEL ALLOWED TO ENTER

Subsequently, key personnel of affected premises will be allowed to enter the cordoned area in order to undertake emergency work and begin salvage. The delay in actually gaining access varies greatly from incident to incident but can be reduced to the minimum by following the requirements of identification and suitable protective clothing as detailed in the following sections.

25.4 POLICE RESOURCES

Police resources are usually severely stretched at checkpoints should the incident involve a bomb. Police need to ensure that only bona fide people are allowed to enter the area, in order to avoid theft, looting or the planting of further devices. There are a great many other people who will also try to enter a devastated area, including unauthorized employees, employees of utilities and artisans of all descriptions, some legitimate and some not.

25.5 GOOD WORKING PRACTICES

The following procedures have become part of many BC plans as 'good working practice' but are certainly not currently recognized by all emergency services or local authorities. It is advised therefore that local authorities and emergency services are contacted to determine what systems are available in specific areas.

25.5.1 Maximum ten key personnel

A maximum of ten members of staff or others will be chosen as key personnel who may enter the site as soon as it is declared safe. As already discussed, an area of major damage may still remain under police control for some time in order to protect it from looting. It is therefore important that all those who represent a business, whether employees, insurance assessors or contractors, have satisfactory identification and authority to enter the damaged site.

25.5.2 ID cards

The ten nominated persons will carry special corporate identification cards, which should include the holder's photograph. These must be worn on outer garments at all times and be readily visible. The team leader should carry a letter of authority, written on company paper and signed by a senior company representative.

25.5.3 Protective clothing

Police are unlikely to admit people to devastated areas unless they are dressed in suitable protective clothing and this may necessitate the use of hard hats, boots and gloves and so on. A supply of protective clothing should be held at various corporate sites and key personnel should also maintain a personalized kit at home. Protective clothing is fully detailed in Section 27.

25.5.4 Mobiles

Mobile radios or telephones can be used and the availability of such methods of communication can be an essential safety measure. However, heavy use of mobiles will mean that a plentiful supply of spare batteries and charging facilities are essential.

25.6 IN THE EVENT OF A MAJOR FIRE

Once the fire brigade has been called, the site and area of a fire is under the direct authority of the senior fire office and police will control the public in accordance with brigade requirements. Once the fire has been extinguished, the site, dependent upon the size, nature and ferocity of the fire, may be:

- handed over to police if there is suspicion of arson
- handed over to the local authority engineers if the building is likely to be dangerous
- handed over to the owners.

There is rarely any rapid notification of which department has jurisdiction, and gaining entry to the premises for the purpose of security and salvage by the company is the responsibility of the BC administrator. It will also be necessary for corporate insurers to be kept informed of the situation as it progresses.

Overview

26.1 DOCUMENTATION BACK-UP

It is probable that, within the foreseeable future, all corporate documentation will either be:

- automatically backed up on corporate computer networks

or

- stored on compact optical disk with duplicates stored offsite

and

- essential original documents stored in secure vaults with electronic or hard copies used as working documents.

This is intended to produce the following results:

- reduce the urgency for salvaged documentation or reliance upon it
- give all departments, even when working at emergency sites, instant access to working documentation via electronic back-up
- reduce the need for departmental staff to be removed from their normal business duties to deal with large quantities of salvaged paperwork.

Together these will permit the quickest return to business functionality and profitability with the minimum non-productive use of staff time.

26.2 SALVAGE MANAGEMENT TEAM

Salvage management is an essential part of the corporate recovery process, but those involved should not be drawn from staff employed in key corporate business operations. Frequently, security and property services staff are used in this role because of their knowledge of corporate real estate. They report to the BC management committee and their activities are primarily onsite liaison with, and management of, the various commercial site salvage companies, who will:

- assess the level of damage
- ensure safety and security of service utilities
- secure the devastated site
- undertake necessary shoring-up and building safety
- make a photographic or video record of the damage

- inventory the loss and damage
- recover equipment, documentation and other property
- remove, store and reinstate salvaged property and documentation.

26.2.1 Assessment of levels of damage

The first duty of the team is to assess, as far as possible, the level of damage and pass requirements for emergency boarding, plumbing, pumping or other requirement to BC administration. An assessment of the level of building security will also be required so that guards and security equipment can be hired.

26.2.2 Insurance assessors

If insurance assessors have not already attended the site, they should be informed, as a matter of urgency, that the site is about to be disturbed and salvage and removal of property is about to take place. BC control will ensure insurance representatives are given all possible assistance, but the process of salvage and recovery should not be delayed in any way.

26.2.3 Safety and security of service utilities

Damaged but undetected water, gas or electrical services are common hazards and may even become the subject of vandalism. Therefore, while part of the salvage team will manage security of the site by means of contract security guards, they will also assess any damage they may find to service utilities, and inform BC administration of the need for emergency repairs.

26.2.4 Contract guards

Contract guards should be issued with a letter of authority and temporary ID passes to enable them to attend the site, and their details may be faxed as confirmation to the appropriate police station if the site remains under police or fire brigade cordon. Guarding will usually need to operate on a 24-hour per day basis and all guards will need to be issued with full protective clothing by the BC administrator, as it is unlikely to be available from the guarding company unless prior arrangements have been made. It is also necessary for the BC administrator to ensure that, while onsite, the guards have satisfactory toilet and refreshment facilities, shelter and a method of communicating with their employers.

26.2.5 Security of the devastated site

Once contract guards have arrived and been briefed, responsibility for security of the site will pass to them. The salvage management team will also need to supervise the erection of necessary protective hoardings and/or scaffolding to an agreed plan. It is likely that insurance brokers and local authority surveyors will also need copies of plans for proposed hoardings as well as timescales for completion of the work.

26.2.6 Supervision of shoring-up and building safety

BC control may need to appoint structural engineers to assess the level of structural damage and assess and implement the requirement to ensure safety so that salvage procedures may commence. It is important that security is maintained and that any modifications to security procedures or to protective hoardings are agreed with the onsite salvage management representative. All such modifications must be notified to BC control and the company health and safety officer.

26.2.7 Inventory of loss and damage

Once the damaged site has been made structurally safe, there is a need to visually record site details for the following reasons:

- to provide a ready reference of site damage during progressive reclamation
- to assist insurers in and expedite the claims process
- as a detailed record of where equipment, damaged documentation or other items were found, prior to their removal for storage.

It is now common for the company salvage team to video the entire site in detail and include a sound commentary. The original location of items which have subsequently been salvaged has frequently proved to be of importance, particularly where there is a suspicion of criminal involvement.

26.2.8 Recovery of equipment, documentation and other property

26.2.8.1 Site salvage contractors

In the event of a major incident, site salvage contractors are available to supply essential assistance at short notice. The facilities they provide are usually predetermined, dependent on the business to which they relate, and form the basis of an annual contract. The annual fee for such a 'standby' contract is usually low, with the cost increasing upon invocation. Normally available facilities are detailed in Appendix 18, but in brief these include portable accommodation, generators, lighting, pumping and refrigeration, transportation, containers and manpower. Such contractors will assist with the removal of property from the damaged site, under the direction of the salvage management team. The order of salvage will be largely dictated by specific circumstances of the incident and the nature of the business, but the following are common examples:

1 Unprotected documentation (unspecified) will be packed 'as is' into containers supplied by the contractor. The containers will be marked by the salvage management team and the original location noted. The container will then be removed by the contractor for safe storage at their warehouse.
2 Documentation which has been damaged or soaked will again be packed into containers and marked as in (1). The salvage contractors will ensure that all damaged document containers are stored appropriately – charred documents in airtight containers; wet documents to be frozen: this is VERY important.
3 Important documentation which is secure and undamaged will be dealt with as in (1) and removed to another corporate site, as directed by the salvage management team.
4 If vaults or other forms of high security storage form part of the damaged site, they will remain intact and their contents undamaged if left unopened.

They should remain undisturbed until the BC committee can ensure the secure removal of their contents to a place of safety. Provided that the devastated site is suitably secured and guarded against criminal intrusion, clearance of vault storage must remain a low priority.

5 Electronic office equipment is likely to be severely damaged as a result of bombing, fire or water. **NO** attempt should be made to turn it on to see if it works as this can destroy data that may otherwise be recoverable. Damaged equipment should be removed from the site by salvage contractors to appropriate storage where it can be assessed and stored data removed as necessary.

26.2.9 Removal, storage and reinstatement of salvaged property

26.2.9.1 Property storage

As detailed above, the property which is packed into containers supplied by the salvage contractors, will be transported under the supervision of the salvage management team to secure warehousing. It is likely that, at some time, departmental staff will need to attend the warehouse and take charge of their own salvaged documentation. It is anticipated that this could be a very time-consuming process, particularly where documentation is damaged and needs to be reclaimed, copied and filed, prior to transportation to a secure site (see next section).

26.2.9.2 Damaged documentation

Expert assistance is available for the reclamation of damaged documentation, but such specialist treatment is time-consuming and therefore expensive. It is likely to be the responsibility of the departmental head to make a member of staff available, who is able to assess whether the damaged documentation is of sufficient value to warrant the time and cost of reclamation. The following briefly describes the process by which burnt and sodden documents are reclaimed.

Burnt documents are usually retrieved by 'setting' the areas of ash with a varnish and then photographing them. Sodden documentation is usually kept frozen to inhibit pulping and growth of mould. Bundles of documents to be reclaimed are thawed out and immediately separated, treated, dried and photocopied. Neither process would be practical or cost effective for large quantities of low-grade documentation.

26.2.9.3 Other property

Property other than documentation which is also removed to the contractor's secure salvage site, should be retained for inspection by insurance loss adjusters. Items such as PCs and office equipment should not be sent for repair until inspected by insurers.

26.2.9.4 Items of value

Items of value such as pictures, clocks or furniture will also be removed to the contractor's secure salvage site. After informing insurers, BC administration should make arrangements for these items to be taken to suitable restorers without delay.

26.2.9.5 Items housed in safes or vaults

It must be reiterated that items housed in safes or vaults are likely to remain secure and free from damage, although water can seep in. The requirements of individual members of staff must take second place to the continued security and safety of the vault contents as a whole. Opening of vaults at a disaster site should come under the specific authority of BC management and should only be undertaken when the following criteria are met:

1 A safe route to the vault has been made through the debris.
2 Once opened, the contents of the vault are not in danger of being damaged by the surrounding site (that is, large quantities of water).
3 The perimeter of the site has been made secure.
4 There is sufficient security staff available to give adequate protection and a corporate manager is present at all times.
5 There is a suitable method of moving the vault contents.
6 A suitable site for rehousing the contents is available and it has been agreed with insurers.

Protective clothing and equipment for salvage management teams

27.1 SALVAGE MANAGEMENT AUTHORIZATION

The BC administrator should ensure that a pre-agreed number of staff are in possession of corporate identification passes with photographs which identify them as members of the BC salvage team.

27.2 SALVAGE TEAM MEMBERS (UPDATE)

It is the responsibility of the BC administrator to update the list of BC team members when required.

27.3 TEAM EQUIPMENT

The salvage management team will need to be supplied with full protective clothing. This may vary, depending on the nature of the damaged site, but is likely to include the following:

- protective overalls
- heavy duty boots
- leather gloves
- hard hats
- protective glasses and face masks
- heavy duty torch
- emergency first aid pack
- at least one mobile telephone per team onsite with spare batteries
- a video camera for the team member undertaking duties as listed in Part 3, Section 26.2.7.

27.4 TRAINING IN SALVAGE MANAGEMENT DUTIES

It is the responsibility of the BC administrator to ensure that suitable training in salvage management duties is given and that all the requirements of health and safety legislation are met.

Index